Why

# Singles are not Married
## &
# the Married are Single:

*Getting to the Heart of Broken Relationships*

# Mike Marra

# Why Singles are not Married & the Married are Single: Getting to the Heart of Broken Relationships

All scripture is quoted from the New International Version (NIV) Study Bible.

Published by: To His Glory Publishing Company, Inc.
463 Dogwood Drive, NW
Lilburn, GA 30047
(770) 458-7947
www.tohisglorypublishing.com

**Books available at:**

Amazon.com, BarnesandNoble.com, Borders.com, Booksamillion, etc. and other online bookstores.
**Also available at:**
www.whysinglesarenotmarried.org

Cover design by: To His Glory Publishing Co.
ISBN: 0-9-774265-0-5

# Dedication

In loving memory of my dad, Aunt Adaleen, Uncle Joe, Aunt Marie, David Norfolk and Mark Sauer.

*This writing is dedicated to all of you for taking a moment, and getting to the heart of broken relationships.*

# Contents

# Acknowledgements

It would not go without saying that my parents were the most influential people behind my writing. I am proud to be their son and have been blessed with two people who loved each other in good times and in bad. Their example has never been forgotten, nor will it ever be.

A very special thanks goes to Muni Bhambri, Tanya Christensen, Adam Jones and Steve Marra for critiquing this work. You all inspired me with great insights from your several different marital perspectives.

Mary Leathers, a very loyal and caring friend, I thank you for your endless support, enthusiastic attitude, and belief in me as well as this writing. Many times it was your words that put me back behind the computer. Your insight from a single woman's point of view, and the editing process you selflessly took upon yourself is priceless.

Much heart felt appreciation goes to Anne Caffey and *The Wounded Heart Ministry*. There aren't enough words to express how grateful I am for your dedication in guiding me in my spiritual growth. You've helped me unlock the door to my purpose in this life and to fulfill my dreams of being published. It is like they say: when God has something for you to do it is humanly impossible. We need Him all day, every day.

I thank you Mary Ogenaarekhua, my publisher, for all the time that you spent helping me to understand this awesome process of publication, and the words of wisdom you provided. The journey has been an exciting one!

All six of my siblings have been involved in one form or another. They may not know that because we live so far from one another. Nonetheless, I'm thankful for them being there when any of us needed support, or a shoulder to lean on.

The list is endless with the numbers of people I have had the privilege to know, and who have taught me something more profound to become a better person. Thanks to all of you!

Last, but not least, is my Heavenly Father who disciplines, molds, and shapes all of us for a more abundant life. I can honestly admit; *I wrote a book, but God was the author!*

# Before we Begin

It has been a challenging experience to prepare this writing. The scope of the text in this book only scratches the surface of what's being addressed. You'll soon discover that each chapter could be its own book! I am trying to present a "slide show" of the "state of our relationships" as I have witnessed, or experienced, along with countless others. Remember, the underlying topics deal with values and morals from a godly perspective.

I feel it's time to retreat from the intricate study of the human mind and theoretical case studies. We need nut and bolt insight into why we're still single, divorced, or remarried again and again. Both genders of *"mainstream society"* are being addressed with the intention of creating a balance of spiritual and emotional responsibility between a man and a woman prior to, and after, marriage or divorce.

This writing addresses the subtle ruin of the once sacred family unit. It reveals why hopeful single men or women may never get to the altar. Vast majorities of people persist in holding great optimism for love and marriage to one person, yet they seem incapable of sustaining a relationship, or they maintain the wrong type of relationship. Even though division among men and women has surfaced within dating and marriage relationships, every heart continues to anticipate everlasting love.

I am personally saddened by the increasing loss of women's femininity and their God-given roles, and the effect this loss has had on society. Concurrently, I'm dismayed with the amount of passivity, lack of masculinity, and the loss of God-given roles in men. Throughout this book, we will look at some repercussions of our actions regarding the haphazard use of our innate gifts.

My hope is to help each gender realize how important it is to maintain specific innate roles, and to carry them out as God designed in our current marital status. We will look at copious truths, and at a variety of subjects regarding singles, and married or divorced couples. This book advises the reader about family, community, and God. It encounters issues ranging from commitment, roles, finances, sex, femininity, masculinity, and "socially acceptable" practices, to the recognition of spiritual battles within us.

*It is imperative to read the chapters in chronological order. Skipping around may not give you the proper insight into what is being stated because of how the chapters are linked. It's the type of writing you may need to read more than once because of the amount of information. Self-examination is prompted in each section. If some areas are difficult to face, stop and return later. Be advised of sexual discussion.*

# Getting to the Heart of the Story

It seems as though society has lost pride of its nation, family, monogamy, and God. Instead, many people seek a "micro-waved" life of prosperity, and ungodly freedom. We hurt the ones we're supposed to love, and children are the biggest victims. Love-starved adults battle for position with their spouses, and locate opportunities for infidelity, while lonely singles scratch their heads looking for a worthy mate!

Life was given to us in order to love, honor, and respect other significant people around us. The basic rules for relationship have been tampered with dramatically, and have turned into some huge scientific, political, and competitive nightmare. Now, the basic equation, one male plus one female equals one relationship, has changed. As it stands, in many cases, one male plus one female equals two people in a divided relationship, with no common denominator. Instead of being "one flesh", there are "two fleshes" doing as they please, independent of one another.

America shows signs of becoming the modern day Babylon, Sodom and Gomorrah. Each divorce, abortion, gay marriage, wife swapping computer site, cohabitation arrangement, unethical media program, and every passive parent refusing to discipline their child, are the primary avenues reducing the strength of our nation every day. Confusion has set into the minds of many men and women, and they do not know which direction to turn.

Maybe you recall, as a teenager or shortly thereafter, daydreaming of your handsome husband or beautiful wife. You were engulfed with a superb feeling of love and hope! It used to be that the majority of men respected women and women adored their men. Most people displayed honorable moral and character. They respected another person's dignity. It was all part of the "American Dream" with the vision of having a white picket fence and kids running around in the backyard chasing the dog. Relationships were steeped in romance, with men being men and women being women.

We were told in the 1960's and 70's that our lives would be much easier and more stress free with the advancement in new technologies. We were led to believe more time would be available to us, and money would no longer be an object.

Virtually, we should have it all together by now. Our lives ought to be stress free with lots of time and gobs of money to burn! The opportunity to love and be loved should be at an all time high with the amount of prosperity and personal availability, right? Why then, are so many people stressed out, unhappy, working paycheck to paycheck, and having marriages fall apart so rapidly and repeatedly?

With all of the stress in our daily lives, from overwhelming expectations in the workplace to unrealistic expectations in our relationships, America and other societies continue to weaken as love is being put aside. All of the technology, knowledge and equal opportunity in the universe will never keep America or any other country afloat as a mighty nation. Strength of individuals, communities, and nations begin within the family.

With all of this turmoil around us, we definitely have a need for *God, love, family,* and *patriotism.* These ingredients are the foundations of a great nation. They're the power to defeat the enemy. They provide a desire to thrive toward oneness and uniqueness. Our strength and foundation for values, morals, passion, and prosperity are found within these virtues.

Because we are designed for relationship, and the need to love one another *selflessly*, we now ache and grieve for attention and the feeling of love due to our *selfishness*. The yearning for love stems from coast to coast, and throughout the nations. True love is difficult to achieve because our "advancements" have actually divided, hurt, and depressed people beyond our comprehension.

The world has turned its back on God and what He intended life to be! Yet, there are myriads of reasons, excuses, and blame for the high rates of divorce and singleness.

In a moment, we'll confront many of the issues already outlined. For now, I realize many born after 1970 may have never experienced the "simple life." Their only acquaintance might be the pressure, tension, and grief of modern day relationships. Sadly, these individuals may have never understood or witnessed true love and commitment.

This message comes from vast experience, endless spiritual counseling, and numerous observations and insights. I pray you receive this awakening *in love,* not condemnation. We have all contributed to the state of our world, including myself! Hopefully, this will assist many to avoid unhealthy and ungodly patterns in relationships, and will help to prevent children from being victims of adult issues.

# Chapter 1

## Meet Mom, Dad and the Concept of Love

The Great Depression and WWII had to be the two most difficult times of the twentieth century to live through. My parents were raised in the midst of those very rough and treacherous times as children and teenagers. Both sets of their parents were Italian immigrants who had enough struggles of their own, let alone any added pressures. They persevered in the name of freedom and for a better life for future generations.

My dad distinctly remembered WWII. He was at the attack of Pearl Harbor on December 7, 1941. He witnessed Japanese attack planes bombing and creating havoc all around him that dreadful Sunday morning. The stories he told up until his last days were intense and tear jerking. He had countless recollections of how he lost close friends because of the bombing attack. Many times those men were no more than 20 to 30 feet away from him. Another time, he spoke of almost losing his life, when his friend saved him from being stabbed in the back.

Somehow he survived, and battled for a total of six years in the U.S. Navy. When the Navy asked him to re-enlist again, after 17 battlefronts on the U.S.S. San Francisco, he politely bowed out, as their intentions were to send him back to another war zone. I'm glad he retreated because he didn't know how to swim! Nevertheless, the U.S.S. San Francisco was one of two ships most decorated (*the greatest number of battle zones*) during WWII.

After making it through that turmoil, he returned to

his hometown and started a service station business. His two brothers, who also served in WWII, joined forces with him in partnership. However, at this point in time, my dad was still single.

Dad met his future wife on a blind date. Her brother instigated the rendezvous. It took him almost six months to call her back! However, at the age of twenty-three, this very pretty woman graciously walked down the aisle in her radiant white wedding gown. She married her twenty-nine year old Prince Charming! In 1950, people married much younger, but the divine plan for my parents took a bit longer to unfold.

Dad used to say, "I would've stayed single my whole life if I had made it to thirty!" Sure pops, how do you explain seven kids and fifty-three years of marriage then? I think he was being facetious. Both he and my mother had a lot of unselfish love to give away. Mutual respect, trust, honor, and submission fueled their relationship.

After my parents married, they drove cross-country from New York to California for a thirty-day honeymoon escape. My dad told his new bride to pick any city along the way to stop and settle in. Before you knew it, they had experienced California, and the ride back to upstate New York! Their car was without air-conditioning and the speed limit was laughable! I guess you'd say they were "roughing it" compared to today's standard.

These two people cared about *each other*, not about the things they had or didn't have. They were on their way to building a life together! "For better, or worse, till death do them part." That was stamped in their heads and on their hearts from the day they married until my dad passed away in June of 2003.

Most people dream of being married to the same person their whole life. People say this all the time, even if they've been married several times before. In my parents' case, it came to pass, but it didn't happen just because they wanted to be married one day. First, they got to know each other over a two-year period of time, and became friends. They also agreed that marriage wasn't a trial run. Then, they became *committed* to one another.

The magic formula for their success required much work, sacrifice, faith and love. I'm sure they experienced the temptation to run from it now and again, but they persevered with character. All the trials, changes, and pressures molded them together into "one flesh," rather than them throwing in the towel and becoming two.

My mother was a stay-at-home mom. Meals were always on the table. Clothes were neatly pressed and clean. Prayers were said every night and church attended every Sunday. The house was usually in order... there were only seven children to contend with! Nonetheless, her sacrifice, hard work and commitment never faltered. She was a model of strength and morality for her family. Overall, mom and dad pressed forward for a better tomorrow.

## How tough is your Love?

Upon returning from their honeymoon, my dad and two brothers started building a business from the ground up. This not only included the clientele, but these guys literally constructed their service station! The business became the most successful service station in the area. Three families, totaling nineteen people, were fed from the trade for forty-two years, and everyone was satisfied materially.

19

Once the building was up, these three brothers helped each other build homes for their families. I think they were determined, and had goals to pursue in their hearts and minds. They didn't wait to win the million-dollar lottery because of experiencing so much grief as young men. Nor did they feel entitled to preferential treatment because of their heroism in war. Their constant devotion to provide and conquer was at an all time high. The love they had for their families was being executed for the welfare of everyone.

Their God-given, innate talents and determination were chugging along in unison. Their masculinity was self-expressive, which in turn, provided roofs over their family's head. *"That's the way it was"* and *"That's the way it should be!"* Men were men, and women loved them for being what they were created to be.

Men loved their women because these women utilized their innate talents and gifts to help fill the voids men were incapable of. Not only did men work in unison with each other, but women worked in unison with men on the other side of the coin. This brought completeness to each individual with a sense of purpose, belonging and accomplishment.

Meanwhile, residing in an apartment, with first child in hand, my parents' house was being built. It went up a section at a time, using a construction loan to finance the endeavor. The first task was to pour the foundation. Upon its completion, an appraiser inspected the work. Whatever the foundation appraised for, the bank loaned that amount of money to my father, using the foundation as collateral. Whatever that money allowed for construction, the appraiser came back for another inspection. More money was lent on what was completed. This process continued until the house was finished.

As soon as the roof was completed, my parents moved into their new abode. I'm sure they were very excited to be a part of the American Dream! Well... almost. There was one thing missing that most people would find quite necessary... WALLS! Yeah, the house was without walls. The framing was completed, but the drywall was not installed yet. The bathroom only had bed sheets around its perimeter for privacy! Who in their right mind?

It has to get better from here, right? Well... there was something else going on with mom while the interior was being completed. She was pregnant with child number two! Maybe you can see where I'm headed with the moral of this story.

This woman was faithfully dedicated to her husband... no matter what! It was the decision she made, the vows she kept, the self-sacrifice of love she offered, along with the respect and honor she had for her husband as he worked fearlessly.

I'm sure mom was ecstatic when the drywall was finished and she could live under normal conditions. But, that entailed many years of watching her husband work 12 to 18 hours a day, including weekends. Once he got home, work continued as he put up the walls. He *also* stuck to his vows, was self-sacrificing, and deprived himself of sleep, rest, and relaxation.

His masculinity, her femininity, their unselfishness, commitment, and like-mindedness resulted in many decades of marriage. They experienced the dream many of us have today. It's refreshing to know it's possible for marriage to last for a lifetime, even with major struggles. Then, they enjoyed their "Golden Years" fulfilling other dreams.

What awesome commitment, love, remarkable loyalty and dedication. As you may have seen, love isn't a *fuzzy, warm feeling*. Love is a *decision* to put self aside for the welfare of another. I believe Christ did that for all of us too!

## Healthy childhood Memoirs

I haven't easily forgotten my childhood. Not because it was difficult, abusive or harsh, but because it was memorable, safe and enjoyable. I consider myself one of the fortunate few able to experience a fulfilling chapter of life. My childhood was built on a foundation of morals, values, love, and the discipline that came along with it.

The "top ten" reasons I feel fortunate is because of my mom. She worked outside of the home when children *weren't* involved. After her first pregnancy, she never left the house to help "bring home the bacon." It was agreed upon that the kids needed constant nurturing and attention. I'm sure if dad needed financial assistance, he would've asked.

Nonetheless, she had much greater responsibilities to fulfill. She was the CEO of her home. Her duty was to raise the kids and support her best friend by keeping him happy and healthy in order for him to provide. It was an accepted "season of life."

There were a total of nine people residing in my parents' house: five females and four males. You would assume there had to be at least two or three bathrooms. Actually, there was only one! Everyone got along well with the accommodations. My four sisters shared a bedroom and I shared a bedroom with my two brothers. Because we knew nothing different, we learned a little sacrifice and unselfishness. Thank God my parents knew about sacrifice. It would've been awfully difficult to raise children without it!

Mom always protected her baby in the womb. She never smoked or drank in or out of pregnancy. She exercised to Jack LaLanne everyday. Her goal was to bring healthy children into the world because health was the first gift she could give to them.

We usually waited to eat until dad came home from work. Many times it was eight or nine o'clock at night! It was time to praise mom for her cooking abilities and thank God for our supply of food. Dad was proud to see the fruits of his labor. The dinner table was the sanctuary of the family. Everyone was present and conversation never lacked!

The main objective of sitting together as a family *was* conversation. Our discussions disclosed what was happening in our lives. Our parents heard gossip, first hand, and intervened if necessary. Eating together brought support, confessions, unity, and sometimes the feeling of wanting to terminate a tattletale!

Today, many families are strangers under the same roof. There's no common time to gather and talk. No one knows what's going on in anyone's life. Parents and children are busy with their own problems. Fast food facilities are visited to cure hunger pains. Realistically, separation of family begins by not having conversation at the dinner table!

Sunday's agenda was an important aspect of our family's intimacy. We all dressed up and went to church. It made us kids feel proud and more mature. Sunday was the only day of the week mom's husband was allowed to break speed limits and run red lights. She had to be at church on time! It was the only day of the week mom's kids wished her husband would slow down and pay attention to the traffic laws!

I know this all sounds outdated, but believe me, a lot of life was going on. There was trouble at school, backyard brawls, trying to get away with things that were off-limits, dating problems, communication gaps, style differences, and so forth. The difference back then compared to now is that there was *honor* and *respect* for your parents.

If mom said, "Wait until your father gets home," an evacuation plan started before he arrived! That was healthy! Discipline was coming to correct a possible disaster. Children want, need, and value discipline when it's properly disbursed.

Fortunately, I witnessed only one argument between my parents. It wasn't a pleasant feeling. I remember sensing insecurity and division in my bones. I recall seeing my dad on his knees begging for forgiveness. His pleading alleviated the case! He took blame and would've done anything to keep the peace.

This event ended up a healthy one in my eyes because I saw resolution and the importance of a woman to a man. Besides that, I don't remember one time my father left the house and didn't kiss my mom good-bye!

Things weren't always perfect growing up. Even so, the battle of the sexes was null and void in this home. I was privileged to witness the cost and rewards of love. My parents' hardships never became a threat, an escape, or blame to end a marriage. It was their lifelong gift to their children. Their positive influence was an awesome example of *love in action*.

So, there it is. Our journey begins with a tale of an old-fashioned family unit. We've witnessed courage, character, sacrifice, romance, long-suffering, patience, hard work, unselfishness, dedication, frustration, perseverance, misery and love. *It's the secret for lifelong marriage!* How tough is *your* love? Can you play the role intended for you as a single person, a single mom or dad, a married person, or a married person with children? It isn't easy, but *all things are possible with God!*

# Chapter 2

## Caught in the Middle

I was born in 1956. Active military duty began in 1975 with the U.S. Naval Seabees. I was raised to attend church, to have a good work ethic, know the benefits of discipline, and to understand the roles of a husband and wife. My "dream girl" was someone pretty in my eyes, fun-loving, and family oriented. She was sexually innocent and had the desire to bear children.

After surviving boot camp and Midway Island, the Philippines became my destiny in 1977. Since the Filipino and Italian cultures are both family-oriented, I seemed to relate well with most of the women there. In the meantime, the U.S. had moved along without me for four years. I received my Honorable Discharge in 1979. Now, at twenty-two years of age, a decision had to be made for my future.

I decided to attend engineering school at Northern Arizona University in Flagstaff. It was a beautiful campus and I easily made friends. I dated a few girls my freshman year, but things seemed different than my experience overseas. It was also different from what my parents had told me to expect from a woman when I was growing up.

Perhaps these women were solely interested in attaining their independence rather than a relationship. Nonetheless, it became more difficult to be part of their lives due to their focus on receiving an education, continuing on to graduate school, and making their fortunes.

After a year in Flagstaff, my transcripts were sent to Arizona State University in Tempe. School was more intense and I had little time to date anyone. However, thoughts in the back of my mind said, "When I graduate, my 'dream girl' will appear and we'll settle down." My best friend accomplished this and my turn was coming.

### When it rains, it Pours

Graduation day came in December 1983 at the age of twenty-seven. A great job opportunity led me to California as an Electrical Consultant. I drove a 1978 Camaro Z-28. It was in cherry condition and always got the "look" from car enthusiasts.

One day, I called my dad to get his opinion of trading in my car. He supported the idea. So, after several more weeks of debating it in my mind, the trade was made for a new 1984 Trans-Am. This car was pretty, but I still kick myself for trading in the "Z!"

After nine months of residing in my apartment and two days of having the new car, a girl appeared for the very first time. She watched me wash the car and asked if I had eaten. My reply was, "no." She insisted to cook a steak dinner! So, we shared stories, ate and saw a movie. It was enjoyable, but a new job was waiting for me in Atlanta.

The next day, there was a knock at my door. Upon opening it, another girl was standing there in a bikini! She asked if I'd join her and six girlfriends at the jacuzzi. Would you have refused? Nonetheless, I was beginning to wonder what was going on. I never linked any of this to the cars because they were equally as nice. I kept thinking, *"When it rains, it pours!"*

The following day there was one more knock at my door. It was another girl who actually came over to *borrow sugar!* At that moment, I knew it was all about the car. I hadn't met anyone in nine months. Then, within three days, I was "blessed" with eight or nine women!

The first girl, who made dinner, was trying to convince me of how much we had in common. She insisted to go back east with me. I knew her three days! She cried in my car for forty-five minutes. I was trying to leave town and couldn't believe this. I was flattered with the female attention, but something wasn't right. It wasn't about me, but a car.

I noticed in Atlanta, women were very pretty, hospitable and competitive. It was heaven for a single man back then. My goal wasn't to see how many girls I could get in bed, even though guys were bragging about their "successes." The odds back then were said to be seven women to one man. It was easy to have multitudes of girlfriends.

I quickly noticed that many of these women weren't "wife material." Believe it or not, I left after three years because women were "too easy," and the male ego was too far gone. There was certainly a quantity of women, but a lack of quality.

Many men took advantage of free sex with the ratio in their favor. They disrespected women and got away with it. This was disturbing to me because women started to advance men sexually. They believed this is what *all* men wanted. The fabulous Sexual Revolution was peaking as women not only lost their virginity; they also lost respect from scores of men at a rapid pace.

The next thing cropping up was concern over the AIDS epidemic. It slowed the onslaught of promiscuity. You'd think it would have scared people back into monogamous relationships, but morality was too far-gone. Today, with multiple strains of STD's, the lack of self control continues to grow.

## The sea of Confusion

The reason these stories are being told is to exhibit the contrast between my childhood expectations, morals and values with what's really out there. I, like many, were *"Caught in the Middle"* of a moral dilemma. Drastic changes occurred during my military and college tours. It took several years to digest the altered lifestyles.

I remember fighting with myself and had to re-evaluate what I was taught. Things like how to treat women and be the masculine figure in a relationship. None of my values were popular anymore. My dreams of having a family were disintegrating. I felt sub-human to a gender that was recklessly dissolving. I thought, "Where does a *good man* fit into society anymore? There surely aren't any prospects left with my values."

At thirty years old, my life was a mess. I was caught up in a sea of confusion. One particular reason was because I had not yet experienced the genuine love of a woman. Fortunately, God made His distinct presence known to me at this time. To my surprise, He started to love me more than ever imaginable. It was, and still is a mystery, but very real. It's my relationship with Him that's taught me more about discipline, love, and relationship than anyone in the human realm. My parents showed me the outward expression of love, but *God awards the inward peace to achieve it!*

He places power within us to fight our spiritual battles and to conquer internal conflict. In my case, I chose seven years of counseling over an eighteen-year period to do so.

I never quit because it's our godly responsibility to renew our mind. That is, to stop programming it with sex, drugs or greed, and to replace it with simple morals and truth.

The plan for my life began to unfold with my interpretation and experience of the woman's movement. Hopefully, this book will allow God to help straighten up your internal conflict. *"For I know the plans I have for you, declares the Lord, plans to prosper you and not to harm you, plans to give you a hope and a future"* (Jer 29:11).

## Speaking of internal Conflict

When problems exist in a relationship, most people try to fix the problem. But, they focus on the issue. The issue might be money, promiscuity, careers, kids or many other things. What needs understanding is that the issue is not the problem! We (the problem) stand in front of the mirror and do not know how to deal with the issue. The issue exists because of unresolved internal conflict. The internal conflict needs healing. *The issue will resolve... once the problem* (us) *deals with the conflict* (emotions).

Instead of facing our conflicts, we blame others, or destroy a marriage. We move to the next relationship with the same issues and ruin it. Then we hear stories of blame when the storyteller is in their fourth marriage! Something doesn't make sense and the person hearing the story should wonder... what is this person's internal conflict?

Nonetheless, two single people of the opposite sex marry, either being emotionally whole and spiritually healthy, or emotionally hurt and spiritually unwholesome. They conceive a baby and when it is born, so are two new parents.

Child rearing and belief systems should have already

31

been discussed before marriage. Unfortunately, many couples don't discuss this, and end up single again because they never talked about these subjects. Nevertheless, most new parents will try to avoid the mistakes made by their parents, and make adjustments in raising their children.

Simultaneously, their children are influenced with the values, morals and internal conflicts of each parent. It's imperative for mom and dad to realize that their lives have changed again. There's a higher level of sacrifice, commitment, and selflessness required because of a new life in their marriage.

There are natural progressions of relationship to help eliminate our selfishness. Healthy phases must be experienced to become less focused on self so that we can better serve the needs of our loved ones. Becoming whole is the personal responsibility of each individual.

Being single is all about personal goals and desires. Dating is the learning stage of sharing interests, doing nice things for our honey, and adjusting to their needs out of love. Engagement is a step toward building a life together, sharing our dreams, and letting the other person know we are willing to love them unconditionally. Marriage is the ultimate commitment: working as a team in our proper roles and making sacrifices to help secure our spouse's world with us. When parenthood arrives, things should become much less important to self, while making bigger sacrifices for the children.

As we're well aware, this isn't what's happening. We are experiencing births out of wedlock with no commitment, visitations to sperm banks in order for mom to have a child and raise it alone, or divorce: all contributing to greater than 60% of children living under the roof of one parent. Then we allow daycare or grandma and grandpa to raise a child while mom and/or dad are at work.

From all of these situations, the only people sacrificing anything for the welfare and well-being of the children are grandma and grandpa! Selfishness is often rampant in marriages because most people are emotionally hurt and spiritually unwholesome.

On the other hand, I applaud the many hardworking moms and dads, married, divorced or widowed, who take extreme interest in their child's development, and who do their best to give them a better life. They instill morals and values needed to make it in the world around them.

The pressure on good parents to raise a decent individual, let alone the pressures on a child today, can be extreme. The numbers of parents who have "learned to let go" of their duties by not properly raising their children, are tormenting the devoted parents who are raising their children in love and discipline. The underlying reason is because the irresponsible parent is only concerned about himself or herself due to the amount of internal conflict they've always avoided.

# Chapter 3

# The Roll of Roles

What is a role anyway? My rendition simply stated: *It's an innate trait created within each gender to execute.* The masculine role of a man is being the hunter, pursuer, protector and provider. The feminine role of a woman is being a nurturer, caregiver, emotional support system and intuitive partner. Purely, she's altruistic by nature, she's a child's mother, and she's a man's strength.

The first relational virtue we need to carry out is our assigned role as a male or female. We can't experience life-long relationship unless roles are agreed to. Denial of this truth is the first and last step to destroying any dating or marriage relationship. Allowing *"roles to roll"* wherever they land is fatal. Satan loves to extinguish intimacy by subtly annihilating the role we were assigned.

The deterioration of gender roles has arrived due to the lack of values and morals. More plainly stated; Satan is having a heyday, blinding the conscience of millions of people who are proclaiming they are godly or good. He robs passion from individuals due to the fear of consequences that might be faced if they aren't being politically correct. He uses political correctness to weaken the roles of men and women.

At the age of fourteen, I approached my mother doing a laundry. She was always doing a laundry! For some reason I asked her this question, "How come you and dad aren't divorced?" Where did that come from? I had never known a divorced person and probably had just learned the word to expand my vocabulary! I will never forget her response. She said, *"Your father knows his role and I know mine."*

From the day she answered my question until I was thirty-two years old, I laughed profusely at her reply. I thought my dad brainwashed her a bit or that her naivety was totally out of control. Nevertheless, the statement remained in my subconscious mind, because deep down, I believed in my mom's profound wisdom. There was a powerful truth constantly speaking to my spirit.

Unfortunately, the world was falling away from her theology as it was being pulled into a new dimension of twisted truths. There was constant turmoil within me that battled right and wrong, but the power of the mass media and peer pressure was much too great to bear. Beliefs were changing rapidly, and for the worst.

With the tide of unsuccessful relationships at thirty-two, I finally realized, *God created both a man and a woman with distinct roles.* The roles are different, both roles are unique, and both roles compliment each other for the sake of the other person's welfare and happiness. You can go as far as saying, *roles are imperative for the creation of intimacy, closeness, unselfish support of another, and for a bond between a male and a female that no other human can break. Without roles, there is no relationship!*

## Rolling into Space

It must have been rather important for a man and a woman to have distinct roles, or they would've never been invented! Looking at society today, roles, femininity, and masculinity are confused. We need to realize the affect this has had on each gender's *"space."*

When the women's movement emerged in the 1960's,

it helped modify the roles of women in society. Much of it was needed. I thought women's new found autonomy meant they would be more self-sufficient until their "Prince Charming" arrived. I thought it meant they would bring additional wisdom and experience to the table of relationship. In turn, a man and a woman would be able to celebrate their wholeness in marriage with more love, and with higher levels of mutual respect and understanding.

Sadly, my thoughts were off target a bit. After embracing some of these new freedoms, I saw many women stretching them far beyond their state of elasticity. For instance, it's hard for me to understand why scores of feminists want to pursue a man's role. They're unable to experience life to its full potential. Their peace is robbed from them due to the constant battle of trying to be something they aren't meant to be. What's so enticing about a man, that makes them strive so persistently to be as "equal," and forfeit their gift of femininity?

I never liked school growing up. My dad used to tell me, "Look, ya have to be there anyway, so, why don't you take advantage of the opportunity to learn?" Perhaps this is relevant here. "Look, you're already a male or female, so, why don't you take the opportunity to enjoy your God given gifts?" It is much less stressful!

As time passed, a "man's space" that he occupied for centuries was "invaded." Much confusion and influence was induced into the minds of countless good men and women. In essence, we told our Creator, "NO," to what His purpose and plan was for us as males and females. We successfully began to hurt ourselves, and the heart of God.

Have you ever seen the email with one electronic

37

box above the other? The one on top has countless knobs and buttons. It is labeled *woman*. The one below has an on/off switch standing alone and is labeled *man*. It's funny when you see it because of its truth. Men are simplistic, and would like to have some space of their own. The constant pressure of feeling "their space" has been invaded in one form or another, overwhelms them.

Most men willingly give women their space. They aren't interested in a woman's space (*female bonding time*) because they still seek their own space (*male bonding time*). It's healthy for a man or a woman to be themselves in an environment not conducive to ridicule from the opposite sex.

If I wanted to play on a woman's softball team, and pursued every avenue to make it a reality, I have created turmoil, uneasiness and tension not only between myself and the team, but among the female gender. Plus, it doesn't *look* or *feel* right! If a woman pursues to play on a man's team, the same occurs. Hence, gender conflict might arise. I am not referring to kids at play.

With a man, if he feels a woman is always looking over his shoulder and into his personal or professional life, *he may become extremely passive in order to avoid gender conflict*. This passivity may cause a man to suppress his emotions, and later become aggressive. In extreme cases, his aggression toward society, in one form or another, could be enacted if he feels his dignity, value or worthiness has been defiled.

Hopefully, we have seen how femininity may become injured if a woman forces herself into a man's role, and how masculinity is damaged by passivity taking a grip. I believe we have rolled into each other's space a little too far, and we need to back up some. Everyone needs space at the mall, in the locker room, in competitive sports and the like. It would allow us to function the way God ordained it to be!

## The invention of Roles

We need to understand where roles originated so we can grasp the importance of their function, and allow ourselves to live in better harmony. If we look at Adam and Eve for a moment, I think we will discover something extremely interesting.

After Adam and Eve disobeyed God, three things occurred. First, God cursed the serpent and the ground. He *did not* curse the man or the woman. They received a *consequence through God's judgment* for their disobedience.

Secondly, God said to Eve, "*... Your desire will be for your husband, and he will rule over you*" (Gen 3:16e). God was saying that her sexual desire would be for her husband. God knew that Eve's other fleshly desire would be to control Adam, so, He emphasized to her, *"he will rule over you."*

Nonetheless, Eve wasn't to rule over (*control*) Adam. God gave her a "direct order." This doesn't say that Adam was to control Eve either! A husband's headship is over his wife, and God's headship is over her husband. There's a *"chain of command"* to follow!

Finally, God said to the man, "*Cursed is the ground because of you; through painful toil you will eat of it all the days of your life*" (Gen 3:16j). God knew a man's flaw would be to blow off work and responsibility, so, He emphasized to Adam there would be "painful toil," or labor, in order to provide for his family. These were the *consequences* of Adam and Eve's disobedience, *not a curse.*

39

Maybe we've realized that *God* ordained the roles of man and woman. In the verses outlined above, does anything else seem peculiar to you? Well, in today's world, *we have reversed the roles that God ordered!*

Looking at society today, some women seem to be in control at home and toiling the earth outside of it. As a result, a woman's sexual desire may not only be for her husband as God intended. As for the man, he's neglecting his responsibility to labor, while his wife is being the provider! Because of his passivity, he relinquishes his godly headship of the family, and as a result, surrenders his God given roles. The conclusion to all of this is that, *man is in rebellion against the judgment placed upon him, and the woman is in rebellion against the judgment placed upon her!*

Hopefully, we realize that most men seek more femininity in a woman than masculinity, and most women seek more masculinity in a man who isn't passive. Until we own up to this truth, and for roles to operate properly, singleness will remain a competitive nightmare due to the amount of pride, past hurt, or rejection.

This same truth affects marriages. It seems that many spouses don't take their roles seriously enough, nor do they mutually agree upon acceptable boundaries in many areas. Each partner seeks to have their unique needs met through their spouse's innate gifts. However, no unity or dependence upon each other exists. Instead of selflessness, pride will rule, and a broken relationship may be the result.

# Chapter 4

## The "Shock and Awe" of Lost Roles

Not long ago, the majority of married men went to work and provided for their families. They were engulfed in every career suited to their natural talents or abilities. If this wasn't the case, men and their wives, appreciated being fortunate enough to have work in order to provide for the family.

Moms were mostly raising the kids, taking care of their husbands, and performing many other vital duties within the home. Men, as a whole, were operating in their innate roles, and thus, never had anything to prove to a woman. Women were operating in their innate roles as well and never had the need to prove anything to a man.

When roles were being played out properly, she was able to provide comfort to her husband, while he was able to provide materially. His burnout came from working outside the home. Hers came from being at home, but part of her burnout was preparing meals along with caring for the kids. She knew her presence was priceless and so did he.

As women have validated themselves in the workplace, there has been a tremendous sacrifice of family values and traditions. Men, in turn, have been confused. There's a desperate heart cry for this idiocy to stop within so many souls of each gender. The loss of relationships, marriages, femininity and masculinity is horrendous because of it. The callused soul developed in each person will take much time and effort to heal.

The subtle elimination of roles snowballed with the "shock and awe" treatment. One day, women were feminine and supportive, while men were masculine and protective. A few days later, women went to work, men stayed home. Selfishness arrived along with uncontrollable kids. We were shocked in the beginning and now it's "normal?"

As mentioned earlier, my parents were the epitome of two people playing out their roles. Each individual felt purpose and belonging. With this in mind, let's travel back to when marriage was more successful than not. Then, we'll discover some issues that have led to broken relationships in the next chapter.

## The way things used to Be

Men used to go to work "bumping heads" with other men. They'd return home to their loving wives who offered emotional support, a good meal and physical affection. In return, their husbands were anxious to provide security, love and protection.

Once rejuvenated, a man revisited the working world, ready to pursue the next highest position in the company. Other men stood up to the cause, and the best man won without any hard feelings. There may have been disappointments, but that was the name of the game and how it used to be.

This cycle continued. However, at the end of the day, men weren't thinking of emotional wounds they may have left in another man's soul because of a healthy disagreement. This trait was perfectly designed to keep men motivated and persistent in their desire to provide. They were (*and are*) capable of expressing themselves to other men without holding grudges too long. Walking in different directions was (*and is*) usually their remedy! If emotion ruled them, they would not have been as assertive in their cause to feed the family.

In the meanwhile, women protected their femininity by working positions leaving them detached from "harsh" competition men enjoyed. They had no need to interfere with something that could harm their womanhood. I am sure they thought men were ridiculous in the way they accomplished things, but it got done without emotional harm.

Many women held careers in nursing, teaching, secretarial, and other nurturing or supportive occupations that both genders honored. Men knew they weren't fully capable to provide the level of care a woman could. Of course, exceptions always apply to rules!

In a nutshell, this was basically how men and women allowed each other to perform in the workplace. Women were recognized in the workplace and were appreciated for their contributions, especially in wartime and specifically during WWII. They were moving forward and earning respect because *every* human deserves it!

Remember, the women's movement actually began in the late 1700's. It exploded in the 1960's! Progressively, it led to property rights, education, and employment opportunities, along with divorce and child custody laws by the late 1800's. Then, women organized to fight for the right to vote in 1848 and persisted until 1920. Their successes are well deserved! However, when a woman believes a career is more important than her husband and children in the late 1900's, it's stretching it a bit too much.

### Parental comfort Zones
As we know, marriage was designed for the union of a male and female. Once mom gave birth, until the child was

about nine or ten years old, she was able to carry out her role of child rearing in a God-given *comfort zone*. Her nurturing, emotional and spiritual support to her children was, for the most part, "easy to dispense." As children became young adults and went out on their own, their foundation was set, being weak or strong.

At the age of ten to twelve dad steps into the picture more profoundly to help develop the child. He's more aware of the realities surrounding his children as they prepare to enter the "real world" of negative influence. Thus, his strong voice of correction and discipline are now as "effortless" to him as the mother's nurturing was earlier on.

I believe men were gifted with deeper voices than women to place a healthy "fear of God" into their kids. It helps them to recognize authority and follow guidelines. A man's voice instills understanding and good judgment in a boy, helping him stay away from unfavorable situations affecting his welfare. As for girls, it helps them to learn submissiveness, and keep their femininity and virginity in check.

Hopefully you see the shift of "parental roles" from the feminine to the masculine side. Mom is in her *comfort zone* of child rearing at younger ages because her emotions can be utilized more efficiently. The children occupy *"her space"* where she can persuade them with nurturance and morality that she offers, in developing her children.

Please don't think either parent isn't important to the child rearing process out of his or her own "comfort zone." It's imperative for dad to be involved while the kids are younger, and mom when they're older. Mom's feminine side is more subdued when they're older because it's "embarrassing" for an older child to feel "mothered" in front of his or her peers.

Dad doesn't use his full-blown masculine side when they are younger. If he did use his strengths at younger ages, he'd scare the kids to death! Dad is in his *comfort zone* of child rearing when the kids are older. He doesn't have to walk on eggshells every time he speaks. He receives the child from the mother with emotional and relational foundations. He then, develops the "real world' issues with the child.

Spouses need each other in child rearing as much as in their marriage relationship. The "parental roles" are in full swing and complimenting one another. Children receive full benefit from it, with a desire to be corrected, even when they act in an opposing manner! It's the breaking and reshaping of the unwise child's character that is being rebuilt step by step. There is *nothing* wrong with that!

Unfortunately, we live in a broken society where many moms or dads aren't available to their children. They've left their roles. An absent parent teaches the child how *not* to love, how *not* to be selfless, how *not* to be moral, how *not* to earn a dollar, how *not* to help someone in need, how *not* to sacrifice, and how *not* to be responsible.

Innocent children are being pushed through imperative training periods unattended. They're thrown into a world in which survival belongs to the fittest. I believe our children need mom and dad's presence, along with their love and discipline. Unfortunately, absentee parenting doesn't seem to be working at the moment.

## Choosing between Morals
The first level of "Shock and Awe," with the biggest impact on society, began in the late 1960's. World televised attention ignited the sexual revolution. You know, burning of the bra, sexual equality or freedom rallies, etc. There

was a need for feminists to proclaim "sexual freedom." Contraceptives became easier to attain, from diaphragms to birth control pills. This gave these women the right to choose between two morals.

One moral choice a woman may have made was to have a prosperous and monogamous relationship with her husband. The ability to control the size of families developed. This was the more positive side. The other moral choice was her having the convenience of noncommittal sexual ties out of wedlock with someone other than a husband. This was considered a more negative side.

Over the years "sexual freedom" has crippled both children and adults. Both face STD's, pregnancy and abortion. We're in a predicament and the troubles get bigger, deeper, and *younger* all the time. This is why it's time to speak up.

We need to ponder something for a minute. If men were "sexually free" in the 60's and prior to then, who were they having sex with? A revolution wouldn't have been required if they engaged with everyday women. Life would've been as it is today regarding sex. Do you think, maybe, these guys were overseas in the military, or in college *paying* for these sexual pleasures? Is this what feminists were envious of?

Before the 1970's, people married earlier to satisfy their sexual needs. Morality was more widespread. Nowadays, we hear about people waiting longer to marry and the divorce rate dropping. Is it because we've become more chaste and self-controlled? Well, we know better than that. It actually has to do with cohabitation and having our sexual needs met. "Why buy the cow when you can get the milk for free?"

"*Now to the unmarried and the widows I say: It is good for them to stay unmarried as I am. But if they cannot control themselves, they should marry, for it is better to marry than to burn with passion*" (1 Cor 7:8-9).

# Chapter 5

## Issues Leading to Broken Relationships

Approximately two-thirds of mothers work away from home. When it comes to statistics, it's hard to say if these women are married, divorced, widowed or how old their children are, etc. Nonetheless, we hear a parent or television mom tell their daughter, "You can do anything a man can do." I believe this statement is very misleading to a young woman.

It's logical that never-married females need to support themselves. Some may never want to marry. It's valid for divorced women with children to work. In some cases, it's suitable for both spouses to work in order to survive. We'll deal with all of this later. Right now, let's examine how things have developed in the workplace.

We've seen how men took responsibility in the workplace and competed with other men years ago. Their simple and unique way of relating helped them to achieve their goals. Suddenly, drastic changes occurred when scores of women entered the workplace. Men were no longer "exclusive" in corporate America. Over time and with many trials, men had to learn to adapt to the emotional make-up of women at work, and compete for position with them.

Competing for a position is fine. However, many males have found they have to watch every move they make, each word they speak, and every action they take, in a "space" they felt was once "theirs." If a man unknowingly becomes a target for harassment towards a woman, he may be threatened with a lawsuit. Some innocent men, in their "simplicity" are being hurt by these allegations, just as some innocent women have been hurt by the grip of feminism.

I am sure that there are particular men who reap what they sow. They've been guilty of harassing females in the workplace, both prior to and after these women gained higher pay and position. "Getting even" can be understood at certain levels, but the *home* may reap much grief in the midst of these conflicts at work.

As this "battle" and confusion continue, men have become more passive and absent in the workplace. It isn't because they don't want to be there. They resent the pettiness. What is natural to them is not natural to a woman and vice-versa. The competition between men and women, at work, isn't the type of rivalry men previously experienced. Competition now involves *emotions*.

Have you ever noticed the number of T.V. commercials advertising females applying for college, joining the military, fixing the house, driving the new sports car, having a big office and every other thing known to mankind? Commercials communicate the absence, weakness and needlessness of a man in society!

If you dare to look, it's materializing in the real world. Stop listening to those saying that television has no affect on our children. Adults react to what's on the tube and kids watch more than adults! The point to grasp is this: everywhere you turn, a woman is portrayed as the hunter, provider, pursuer and protector! She doesn't need a man anymore because "*she can do it all.*"

## Where did she Go?

We've briefly approached a basic theory explaining why men are vanishing from their responsibilities. Television, lawsuits and the loss of femininity weakens them. But, what's going on in the home to create broken families?

Problems first began when some women were being called inappropriate names for giving sex to a man out of wedlock. A woman was highly disrespected by some men after sexual relations. Then, scores of men were being classified as chauvinists. These insults had no discriminatory boundaries between a good, or deserving, man or woman.

In order to avoid these complications in marriage, husbands supported their wives' goals outside of the home. I've witnessed several instances where a man did this for his wife or girlfriend. Good men unknowingly contributed to the initial steps of role reversal. Consequently, each spouse's marital commitment began to fade away.

In one instance, a wife started to increase her salary at a rapid pace. Over a short period of time her salary was equivalent to her husband's. As soon as this happened, and without warning, she filed for a divorce! They dated for two years and were married for two years. It may have been better for him to be called a chauvinist.

In another account, a young husband used his hands to build a house for his wife. They had no children and were married two years. His wife made more money than he. One day, she went to work hearing about her girlfriend filing for a divorce. After the divorce, her friend started influencing this good man's wife to leave him!

The friend argued that the wife made more money than her husband. This led to, "why do you need him or the problems?" About four months after her friend's influence, the husband came home and found his wife's belongings gone! Where did she go?

What about an engaged couple considering marriage? Both people are gainfully employed, each making around the $30,000.00 range. The guy is supportive of her. She receives her $2,000.00 annual raise. Everything is good. She has another opportunity within months for a promotion making $50,000.00 a year. That is great. Not long after, an opportunity comes for another $25,000.00 a year! At this point, and after discussing it with her male counterpart, he says, "it's either me or the money."

Of course he lost, and she started making six-figures plus expenses. It all sounds great huh? Well, not long after the big money, she had a nervous breakdown. Hospital bills soared and recovery was long. Was the guy being chauvinistic? No! He saw her priorities, and they weren't conducive to their relationship.

We can't rely on our own strength to gather money. Some people are built to take the pressures associated with it, and others aren't. Many struggle to find wealth, but they are blinded by it. They might be referred to as a good man or woman, but not referred to as such a great mom or dad.

### A glimpse of his wiring Diagram

We begin this tale with a married couple who've experienced many "shock and awe" treatments in society. They have no children and Bob appreciates his wife's financial assistance to save extra cash. However, he still hopes for her presence upon returning home at the end of the day. Many times he sees a very tired wife or sometimes no wife at all. The demand at work has worn her out. When she first married, there was excitement in being able to prove she could "do it all." But, shortly thereafter, it proved otherwise.

Having no children, there aren't many problems going forward unless Bob starts experiencing too much absenteeism of his wife. Everyone has deadlines once in a while, but not *always* for *either* gender. Nonetheless, he seeks support from his wife in order to "knock heads" again the next day. Kids or no kids, he longs for his wife's presence.

Time passes, and his wife doesn't seem to be cooking much. Bob tries to fill in, if he can cook, but he'd prefer a decent meal from his wife. Otherwise, fast food becomes dinner. Then, frustration builds when he goes to bed. His wife went off to "Never-Never Land" before he had the opportunity to get close with her sexually. He was hoping she would be more gracious and thoughtful toward his needs.

The next morning, he's anxious to make love with his wife. Unfortunately, she's getting ready for work or is already gone. He senses more division in the relationship and begins to feel his focus fade on providing for the family. His focus is trying to figure out what's happening and why he's losing his wife. Confusion and frustration become a deeper part of his being. He recalls things being better when she didn't work as much.

On the other hand, she becomes more *emotionally* involved with work as it slowly entraps her. She starts submitting to her company without question, but if her husband asks for something imperative to the marriage, there is conflict. She won't be told what to do. She's "married" to the company and treating her husband without respect.

At this juncture, his innate role, virtues and sense of being are yanked on. These are directly attached to his emotions. In turn, those emotions are tied directly to his wife. His wife is the purpose for him to go out and provide.

Now we come full circle because being able to provide is his innate role! Now we have a glimpse of his wiring diagram!

Once a short circuit fires, he feels less than a man, unworthy, having no purpose, defiled, attacked, or thought of as not being significant or important. The lack of respect is high voltage territory to explore with any man. *It's his number one need!* Sex is second to respect, believe it or not, in his relationship. *It is respect that makes him loving!*

Emotions of anger, fear, rage, judgments, abusive words or acts begin to evolve once a situation surpasses his threshold. Women *are not* to blame for his reactions. They're a catalyst launching the pain of rejection and lack of respect his dad may have reinforced in him!

Programmable infants, toddlers & Preschoolers
It's hard enough for a husband to regroup with being "caught in the middle." What about children? They're getting overlooked drastically in their formative years. No one sees their pain until they rebel. When that happens, everyone's confused. Hopefully, seeing this on paper will help us to feel their pain due to parental neglect.

We'll assume our kids are between birth and five years old. The poor things are literally helpless. They're like a new computer with nothing on the hard drive yet. Someone's going to program them and hopefully it will be a loving and nurturing mother. Their programming remembers the nurturing they received, the tone of voice they were instructed with, physical handling, thinking patterns and many other impressionable principles.

Like a computer, they'll retain programming in their memory. Computers recall only what's required for a specific function at the moment. We are the same. Not until something occurs do we know a person's reaction to an issue. The life they have later is dependant on their initial programming. We react with default memory!

When children get older and need moral discipline, there's a foundation to operate from. If a loving and nurturing mother did the programming, she'll know what version of software she used. Constant upgrades will be required until these kids are on their own.

Upgrading your computer may not respond sometimes due to incompatible software. Guess what? The same thing happens with children. The software has to be compatible or they will not respond. Let's move on to a situation that explains what's being said. And, yes, everything being mentioned has much to do with broken relationships!

### Programming that parents don't Understand

Assume mom and dad work outside of the home. They are professionals and make good money. They have a newborn and call the local Day Care Center. Yes... there's room at the Inn! For me, I can't imagine having a baby inside me for nine months and returning to work six weeks after giving birth. My female side says, "I want to hold and nurture my baby. We experienced a close knit from conception until birth." I am only a guy though. Perhaps my feminine side is way off kilter.

By sending a six-week old infant to daycare, mom may be sending a message of never having interest to bear a child. It's possibly only something she needed to accomplish. I'm sorry, but what excuse or arrangement could be made between a husband and a wife to replace this mother's longing to be with her baby? That's her innate desire and it *will not* change, just like a man's innate desire will *never* change.

Even if this brings discomfort to a mom, it's brushed under the carpet. Nevertheless, her child is now among several other infants who are spreading viruses or sickness. The person watching these children cannot give them the attention they need or deserve. Even if they attempt to provide what the child needs, it's hard to bring comfort.

Biological parents have a hard enough time providing comfort to their own child. Plus, there may be many sleepless nights because of a child who is sick. With only minimal rest, mom and dad go back to work the next day. Who is taking care of the sick child? What kind of day are the parents having at work?

Already the child has experienced abandonment at an early age. This emotion will set deeply into the child's spirit. This, in time, will affect the child at many different crossroads in his or her life. If parental desire to nurture the young child is neglected, can you imagine how rejected the kid will feel as a teenager or as an adult? No one wears a sign saying they feel rejected. Actions define the emotions later on.

Now let's consider the *"programming that parents don't understand."* In many cases, children are left at daycare for the duration of the work day. Caretakers in charge are programming kids with what they feel is appropriate. Memories are burned onto their hard drive through many different experiences. This goes on day after day.

As children become older, parents may try communicating something imperative for their kids' well-being. The kids then may not respond because the first version of software isn't compatible with the new version mom or dad is trying to download. A parent has no idea of what was said or done earlier. So, problems begin to stir as parents feel they have no control.

Other children may be left with a babysitter, a grandparent or another relative. Hopefully, these people use similar software downloads that can be upgraded years down the road. Ideally, it's best for mom to be home with the children at least until school days arrive. It's also important to make sure someone is around when they arrive home again.

There are numerous situations existing and I'm not trying to list them all. We need to understand what's being stated and apply it to our own situations. Some have no choice but to use these available services because of the chaos that's been created.

This addresses those using these services for the wrong reasons, and who *can* be home with their children. Keeping up with the Joneses is not a good reason! If economics are crucial or working is that important, maybe children should have never been considered in this type of environment. It would be better to have one "homegrown" *godly* child under a parent's roof than to have four or five of them brought up under someone else's roof who may not know God!

Separation anxiety truly exists between a mother and child. The spiritual side of the mix always seems to be forgotten. I'm trying to sum up the costs associated with allowing someone else to raise our children. A parent's relationship is vital to their son or daughter. The progression of child separation, abandonment, and rejection creates turmoil for everyone. It flows into society with many socio-economic backlashes.

## Now that they're Older

Our kids are now attending high school and may be involved with sports or after school programs. Many arrive home to an empty house. Now it's time to experiment with things that have been tempting to them for quite some time. Kids are human and will fall off the deep end rather quickly without guidance. There's too much available nowadays to think every child is an "angel." No one is an "angel." Right now we're still mortals!

Teenagers need as much or more attention as before. Some parents believe teenagers are old enough to make their own decisions. Well, it depends on the decision! A dad on T.V. was talking about his daughter going to the prom. She selected a dress having minimal fabric. This decision, he thought, was her choice at fifteen. No dad! It's your responsibility to guide her with decency. You're supposed to teach her how to gain respect from boys. You know how they are!

Recently, at a bookstore, I noticed two teenage girls and how they were dressed. One stood up and I couldn't believe my eyes. She was dressed for the street! Unfortunately, this is popular. Outdoor concerts have girls bare all. Guys lay on them almost performing a marriage act. The worst thing about it is… *they don't care.*

I feel sorry for these kids. I wonder why moms or dads haven't applied wisdom to set their child straight. When pregnancy or all the rest happens, some are shocked while others open the door to abortion with no remorse. This *moral deficit* is reaped from previous generations. My concern for society ignites, because one day, these kids need to protect us, run our schools, governments, and everything else under the sun.

How passive or permissive will these kids be? Their foundation is weak with an inability to decipher what is good, normal or acceptable. How will their kids turn out? What type of programming will they inherit? We might be fooling ourselves to think everything will "work out in the wash." Spiritual laws will inevitably take effect!

Exterminating parental duty is not acceptable. Children of all ages must go through vital learning processes, and that requires responsible parental supervision. In today's world, major detours have been taken around discipline, and they're leading directly to larger detours in the lives of our children.

With a lack of supervision, a child's curiosity becomes more intense, thus, risk taking increases. Families become a little more foreign to each other, as kids get involved with deeper moral issues. Sometimes spouses divorce because of it.

Unfortunately, parents who've sacrificed to raise decent kids have to fight in this moral war zone surrounding their children. Standing ovations are in order for the married, divorced, widowed and single parents who've put *self* aside for their children. Thank you for being sacrificial in the season of life you were assigned. It is refreshing to see children not programmed on "autopilot!"

# Chapter 6

## Super Consequences of Broken Relationships

Ideally, if a responsible man marries, and when kids are involved, he assumes mom will nurture them from birth until school days arrive. Once they're in school, he hopes for her presence to welcome them in the afternoon.

Unfortunately, this value has faded because of financial ambitions outside of the home. In return, stresses, obstacles, and circumstances overwhelm couples due to relational expectations. However, some expectations need to be automatic when our children are involved, along with dad being involved with the kids to help mom!

Money is an issue because of greed in a person's heart (*spirit*), not because there isn't enough to go around. Its glamour has a false image, and marriages suffer the consequences. It's unacceptable in today's culture to be thought of as "poor," even though scores of people suffer with hidden debt on credit cards or home equity loans.

From that, mounting debt leads to bickering and possible bankruptcy. In order to solve these woes, drastic changes must be made, but most people are unwilling. When arguments arise, blame is thrown back and forth, and life becomes unpleasant.

During this frenzy, fears, anxiety and stresses mount. Body chemicals start doing their own thing and become imbalanced. We realize our personality isn't as sweet as it was the previous day. Mild depression sets in. It's easy to get into, we don't realize we're in it, and when we finally do realize it, getting out is a hard job. Consequently, anti-depressants are swallowed. Doctor bills pile up, and all of the subtle heartaches corrupt a marriage relationship.

One initial setup of this misery is purchasing a house. Instead of qualifying with one income, two incomes are required for the biggest possible building. If one person loses his or her job, house payments are set back. Within six months, it's foreclosure time.

I saw this happen in my banking career quite often. To help a bad situation get worse, home equity monies are relatively painless to get, and the money is used to buy a $30,000.00 vehicle with new babies in the house. Banks aren't concerned because they need their quotas met, and it seems that many parents only care about their image.

Planning a family is normally thought of in regards to the number of children and the best time to conceive. Financial planning isn't taken quite as seriously, and the transition from singleness to marriage isn't often considered with regard to finances. Each spouse still operates independent of each other rather than as "one flesh."

So, maybe we've touched on self-induced causes of fear, anxiety and stress. It has nothing to do with anyone else, but with our own inability to handle money. It has to do with selfish gain. In the midst of it all, it's painful to go through constant misery with a loved one while being harassed by creditors. Once again, the relationship suffers and awaits the consequences of a broken marriage.

### A woman's sex Appeal

We'll begin this tale with Bill lying in bed, or preparing for the day as he watches his wife Sandy get ready for work. He sees her apply make-up, select an outfit and spray a favorite perfume. Ultimately, he isn't receiving any benefit from it. It's for other men to admire throughout the day.

Various men may become interested in Sandy's sex appeal wherever she goes. Some only remember their wife in curlers, no make-up, and a nightgown when they left for work. This is acceptable, especially for stay-at-home moms or a pregnant wife. However, Bill subconsciously hopes to receive the freshness and beauty of his wife when he returns home. After all, he witnessed it all day long in other women. Unfortunately, Sandy is tired from a hectic day and may not meet Bill's undisclosed expectation.

Bill may feel that Sandy should intuitively understand his need, and he shouldn't have to mention it. She may notice he is more standoffish. Yet, he doesn't say anything to avoid an argument, or because he feels Sandy won't respect his "trivial" request. Over time he may become frustrated and then releases anger toward Sandy due to his unfulfilled desire.

In Sandy's situation, some men may become more attentive to her in their thoughts or actions. Temptation festers in a few minds while others are frustrated with the distraction. Frustrated men try to avoid interaction with her outside of a specific job requirement. It's handled this way for the sake of their marriage.

Some single men might also find her attractive. They should respect the fact that she's married and stop pursuing another man's wife. Married women should realize they have a husband and keep business the objective day after day, week after week, and year after year. It's hard for a man to avert his eyes away from a pretty woman, but if she's married, and he pursues her, spiritual, emotional and financial prosperity is blemished.

There are other men who feel like a woman's "savior" if her husband travels frequently, or if she is neglected at home. They'll have an affair for as long as they can. If this happens with one woman, it will happen with multiple women simultaneously! He feels important by being attentive to her "needs." If these women have children, this matters not.

As numbers of women multiply in the workplace, along with corporate travel and its destinies, the number of affairs exponentially increases with it. Thus, women have become like men. They now experience the same stresses men have always faced. In order to reduce the stress, an affair away from home may solve everything. Hopefully, women realize this isn't only a man's issue, but a *human* issue.

Nonetheless, Bill notices Sandy upbeat due to the attention she acquires at work. Feelings of jealousy arise in him, as they should. There *is* healthy jealousy for the benefit of sanctity. Remember, scripture speaks of God being jealous. It's because He desires no other gods before Him. A husband or wife can be a jealous spouse because they want no other man or woman before them. It's a powerful "*image of God*" we inherited!

If a man views attractive women all day, he hopes his woman will step up to the plate and look nice for him. If not, he feels disappointment in his gut. Anger or depression may develop because he's *visual*. Conversely, a woman feels the need to be loved unconditionally, but may forget everything her man is tempted with every day. It really needs to be a two-way street of selflessness in order to have our own needs met.

## An affair waiting to Happen

In the previous section, we've witnessed normal human reactions taking place, from getting attention to jealousy. Subtly, this works its way a little deeper when coworkers congregate for a drink before calling it a day.

A collage of married and singles of both genders gather. Things seem innocent, yet feel uncomfortable. Chatting and drinking deepens as each person "zeros in" on who they're most interested in. You know, as though all were single and anxious to meet a cute girl or guy.

This continues repeatedly in the weeks and months ahead. Without notice, the "one-liners" get dropped. First jokingly, with its reception from the other person in shock (even though it's real bait) and then before you know it, the door swings open for an affair.

As this transpires, one spouse is home contemplating where the other is. Little do they know he or she is at a local hang-out with another person's husband, wife or eligible single! Sometimes, an "open marriage" endorses this activity. If so, marriage should have never been considered. Sooner or later someone's going to get real angry.

In time, the missing spouse arrives home. Normally, three reasons exist for being late. Either work tied them up longer than expected, they encountered a lot of traffic, or they accepted an invitation to go out. Advising a spouse you may be late in the beginning is easy; however, when it's frequent, questions need to be asked. Gut feelings surface, but they're avoided, even when knowing something is up. A few "white lies" are delivered, and things are smoothed over until the next time when things become more intense.

If a wife is always waiting home, she may be more gullible in the beginning because she understands his need to "work" late. As time goes on, she might start feeling her husband is cheating on her. If he's the one waiting for her, there's no detour... he'll jump right to the conclusion she *is* with someone! Call it insecurity if you will, but a man desires his wife. His mind is torn apart because of healthy and godly jealousy.

A wife's initial feeling is that her husband doesn't love her anymore. Her "headaches" get worse each night. *The greatest need from her man is love.* She digs for the truth of his tardiness, but he sticks to his story. His feeling, if she's late, is the loss of *respect and honor, which are the two greatest needs a man desires from his woman.* His libido disintegrates.

Honor is *basically* accepting the other person for who they are. So, with the wife being entertained by "co-workers," the husband feels secondary in supplying her needs because of the lack of respect. The final result from all of this is two people losing trust.

When both spouses hold impressive positions outside the home, two masculine counterparts reside under the same roof. Each strives toward individual goals rather than working for the common goal of family values. Things become much more complicated with traveling careers. These situations trigger undisclosed resentment, frustration and anger because it's harder to prove a case.

Some married couples make it through. Some pretend real well, while others detest the lifestyle, and do everything they can to preserve the family. Nonetheless, a husband might be passive with a horrid situation. He doesn't want to rock the boat and create chaos, especially if much financial loss could occur. The couple continues on with a deep loss of affection, while the Super Consequence of divorce lingers.

## Bringing in the Children

I think we understand how subtly and innocently a relationship can deteriorate, with two masculine temperaments under one roof. Right now, it's time to bring children into the scenarios. This is the most tragic part of the whole relational disorder between the parents. If the husband and wife were solely involved in their struggle, that's one thing, but when children are involved, there's a whole new deck of cards being dealt.

For me, the next section reaches deep into my soul. It's the harsh reality children and society face on a daily basis. The reason, I believe, it's so wrenching is because many parents were not prepared emotionally to have kids. They took on the responsibility for something they should've never been given a license to do: *have children without considering the strength of their own relationship and insecurities within.*

No one is ever taught how to have relationships or how to approach a healing process. Only those with an unquenchable desire to be all they can be will achieve their goals. This is true in any area of life we desire success in. Why isn't this marital priority?

Several avenues are available for children to acquire negative influence. It actually starts in a mother's womb as the baby's *spirit* is jarred from verbal abuse and tones of voices it senses. Furthermore, generational "hand-me-downs" from both parents' ancestral lines such as alcoholism, promiscuity, drug abuse or other destructive habits may be "gifted" to the child. Then there's every day life to deal with as they grow.

When a child is induced with neglect, selfishness and rejection from a parent, this input programs the child for a heap of instant trouble, and carries into his or her future.

Add all the other ingredients mentioned above, and there's a ticking time bomb ready to explode. Hopefully, parents will smell the coffee and help reroute their child's destiny!

## When parents aren't Home
In the days of "normalcy," mom would scoot the kids off to school and welcome them back home. Today, a different situation turns society upside down. That is, moms leaving home to work as younger generations find love and acceptance elsewhere. *That somewhere else is anywhere they feel loved and accepted without the fear of rejection.*

Usually, people marry so they don't have to be alone. It's an ill feeling as an adult. Imagine a child who covets hugs and kisses, being left alone. They have more intense feelings of loneliness because they're helpless. We need to put ourselves in their shoes.

As mom and dad bicker over some issues in modern day Babylon, adolescents arrive back home unattended. What are they doing in the world of technology all alone? Are they on a computer or cell phone plotting attacks, or are they involved with pornography or drugs? Teenage sex is easier to accomplish; drinking, or joining a gang are options for these hurt felt children. The lack of a parent's love may drive a child to any of these places for acceptance.

Imagine if the police department calls, a report card reflects poor grades, pornography shows up in the bedroom, dreadful news that our son just shot someone, or that he was killed from a deal going down, or that our thirteen year old daughter is pregnant... we, the parents, are in total disbelief and go into shock! It is tragic, but the consequences are real.

Weren't we children once, trying to get away with all

sorts of things? Why are people shocked because something bad happened to, or with, their child? It's mostly a parent's fault! Their absence absolutely ensured that something would go wrong.

I've noticed parenting techniques today hold the decree that it's better to be a friend than a disciplinarian. God disciplines His children out of love. Are we now disposing of another *image of God* we were created with? Discipline creates unfathomable love.

A super consequence of mom leaving the home is distraught kids. No one taught the children about short or long-term penalties for an inappropriate act they committed. They're never on the hook for a bad decision they may have made. Unfortunately, bad decisions are carried into adulthood because their "role model" has perfected their own mistakes.

It's difficult enough to raise kids when mom and dad *are* home. There are still many influences to be fought and defeated. However, when parents *aren't* home and leave the kids to their own free will, it's nothing but an intense game of "Russian Roulette."

# Chapter 7

## For Better or Worse

It's time for marriage vows to be taken much more seriously. Many working moms are out there because of a divorce. It's impossible for her to be home and nurture her offspring appropriately. Many dads are not living up to their end of the deal, but with temptation all around them, they have to be built of steel not to notice the opposite sex.

Dad needs blinders to focus on his duties. He needs to get more involved in his kid's life and make sure the "privacy act" isn't a law in the home. He needs to suck it up and stop making his kids feel "less than" because of hurts carried forward from his childhood.

Deadbeat dads don't care, single moms can't do it all, nor is there time for many parents to sit and talk with their kids because of other priorities. Many excuses exist out there for neglecting children, while on the other hand, there's no excuse why parents cannot be a positive influence to their child.

Working mothers, married with children, should embrace the fact that the corporate world replaces employees daily. The world still turns and won't miss you if you're gone. *Nonetheless, you'll never be replaced at home where your children and husband depend on you desperately! They desire your presence even if you can't feel it.* No corporation on the planet needs your services as profoundly or urgently than your family. Your vow to your husband was for better or worse, richer or poorer. Men, your vows were the same.

When it comes to a career it's for *better or worse...* hoping it lasts a lifetime. We find a job, work it a short while, and then our boss meets us with a pink slip in hand. What's the first thing we do besides file for unemployment? Clean out our desk, mourn until the pain subsides, feel like life is over, and get mad at our company. After that phase, we look for another job if we didn't already have another in hand! If we didn't have another waiting, we'll find one several weeks, months or even years down the road.

Marriage is supposed to be for *better or worse* for a lifetime. We find a spouse, work the marriage a short while, and then our spouse sends us a pink slip from their attorney. What's the first thing we do besides calling our attorney? Clean out the house, mourn until the pain subsides, feel like life is over and get mad at our spouse! After that phase is over, we look for another spouse if we didn't already have another in hand! If we didn't, we'll find another one several weeks, months or even years down the road.

Hardly anyone treats marriage like a life-long and secure retirement account watching their *interest* build in each other. Rather, most people treat a marriage like a short-term business venture, seeing what they can get out of it until their *interest* changes.

This pretty much sums up attitudes regarding marriage and other relationships today. Once I'm bored and a better opportunity comes along, I'll probably take it. How on earth can people be so nonchalant? People have feelings and those feelings are being exercised through anger, grief, resentment, lawsuits, divorces and a variety of threats that destroy our joy. Then, alcohol and anti-depressants are swallowed even more so after a divorce.

## The blended Family

It seems the "traditional family" has become an array of blended families displaying much lackluster and confusion. One instance might be a single person who never married and settles down with someone previously married one or more times. The divorced person may have children. Or, there might be the situation where both people came from a previous marriage or marriages with children on one or both sides. To make it more interesting, these couples have children together.

Then, we have single women out of wedlock with children, and an absent or unknown mom or dad. They might marry and combine all of their problems with another person who has been married several times. The lists of combinations are endless. These are referred to as the *"blended family."*

Where's the peace? This is complicated to you and I. Imagine how convoluted it must be to the poor kids living it every day! The last emotional understanding they need to realize is why their biological parent was replaced with a stranger. The child needs stability and has already experienced emotional disarray because of parental abandonment.

They're wounded spiritually from the get go because of the rejection they've experienced. As they're forced into a new situation, completely foreign to them, they rebel against the unnatural environment. Not only that, but a child is often used as a pawn between squabbling parents, putting more confusion and guilt on the child.

Conversely, if a widow marries a never married man or another widower, with or without children between them, confusion or guilt doesn't exist! Why is that? Because it was not *willfully* brought upon these people like divorce is. Divorce is a choice often due to *selfishness* and *immaturity*. Successful marriage is a choice due to *selflessness* and *maturity*.

Becoming widowed usually doesn't entail a spouse's choice. The mourning process for the family takes time, but the chance to find love again still exists. In divorce, many unresolved issues might haunt an individual on a daily basis, especially with children involved. Healing may take decades, if it happens at all. The mourning may never cease due to some sort of guilt.

Nonetheless, as the blended family progresses, tricky situations develop. Of course, it's subtle, because one spouse doesn't know the history of the other person's children too well. They'll learn how imperfect things are over a short period of time. Hence, a child could rebel because they want their biological parents back together.

In the meantime, as a child gets older, he or she may express anger in ways that lead to serious legal problems. Once again, it's discovered they may be dealing with illicit or illegal activity. Some divorced couples wish they had remained with their first spouse once they've experienced escalating problems with their new spouse or spouses.

Regarding children, the "new parent" they live with may create trouble due to favoritism or entitlement toward their own child. Children from one parent may have had different social, economic or educational backgrounds. Thus, dissension among the kids may escalate due to an imbalance of parental beliefs and siding with their own bloodline. It's hard to be considered "one flesh" when ideas differ about what's best for *all* the kids.

Love affairs could occur between the kids. Now

you're dealing with sexual desires of adolescents that wouldn't typically develop or be accepted in a traditional family. What do you tell these kids now? It keeps getting more complicated. Problems exist in any marriage! People discover the grass isn't much greener on the other side of the fence.

How about parents who love their child as much, or maybe more than the one with custody? The one with custody remarries under a different roof while the "left behind" parent wishes to have influence on the child. God forbid the problems occurring with children in a cohabitation arrangement! None of this is good.

Usually, these influences become more destructive because competition is the name of the game between the biological parents. The "left out" parent tries to be "cool" and "hip" by graduating the child into things way beyond his or her maturity level. Now the parent seeks acceptance from the child!

In actuality, this competition sets up unfavorable circumstances leading to life changing events for the child. Most divorced parents try to prove their love by showering their kids with money, cars, breast implants, electronic gadgets, big trips, or whatever they feel will make up for their lack of parenthood.

Without thinking of the consequences, each parent grants the wishes of their child for the sake of the child's "happiness." This trend is a cover-up, and isn't what the children want or need. They're hoping for acceptance and love in a stable traditional family!

Overall, divorce has a greater probability of occurring, with these added pressures invading a blended family. Hopefully, we have a clearer understanding of why second, third or fourth marriages have a lesser chance of success than the first one, if healing hasn't been attempted or pursued.

We were designed to live in peace and harmony. Unfortunately, deeper hurt, tension and stress are created for each marriage and cohabitation arrangement that is entered into along life's path. Often our emotions are transferred to our children and it's not healthy for anyone. Maybe this explains part of the physical heart problems we face as a nation. Grief can destroy one's health!

## Reversal of hierarchal Priorities

Due to abnormal circumstances in blended families, there's another source of dissension that either spouse may experience. It actually begins in the dating relationship. We'll call it *"Hierarchal Priorities."* These priorities are necessary in order for our mate to feel loved and accepted during courtship or in marriage. If they're not innately directed, the personal priorities of one person could obstruct or destroy long-term relationship with a prospective, or current, significant other.

What is hierarchal priority? It's simply putting God first by honoring the commandments. If we love our neighbor as ourselves, we'll treat others with respect and kindness. Everyone desires this! Other godly priorities follow, starting with our mate.

When meeting someone new, we aren't sure of where a relationship is headed. The other's career and hobbies may take priority over us for a while. Over time, a transition should occur in which the other person becomes a higher priority in our hierarchy.

Once this happens, the priorities would be God, mate, career and hobbies. In marriage, the hierarchal priorities would be God, spouse, children, career and hobbies. No matter the marital status, God needs to be first and the mate or spouse second. Those knowing how to love always put others first, without totally ignoring their own interests.

If a dating relationship transpires encountering children, *hierarchal priorities suffer.* As time elapses, we recognize the other person's personal priorities. In the case of a woman having custody of a child, her feminine side automatically lessens. She tries desperately to achieve the motherly *and* fatherly duties. Everything is on her shoulders, while hierarchal priorities have no meaning entering the relationship.

It's often difficult for her to be a disciplinarian. Her child zeros in on this weakness. Before long, the youngster plots against her emotions. She starts giving in to the child's rebellion because the battle of discipline was mostly intended for the father. Mom wasn't built for all of this because of her emotional side. If children are submissive to their parents because of discipline, they honor their parents, and realize the authority they have over them. If proper discipline is not accomplished, how would a child realize this?

Most men with custody or visitation rights don't forfeit masculinity to seek their feminine side. Usually, they remain in their "zone" and hope their girlfriend, fast food establishments and daycare will provide the nurturing and care that is needed for their kids. Other men have abilities to nurture their kids, but they are far and in between.

The point being made is that when two people remain married, proper hierarchal priorities have a higher chance of falling into place. When the blended family dating relationship begins, priorities abruptly change, only because they *have to*. God should always remain first, as a parent does his or her best to balance the household.

The person entering a relationship, with children, has a predestined hierarchy. It is *God, career, children, **mate** and hobbies.* His or her mate will never attain second or third place. It's no fault of any single parent trying to raise his or her child. Their priority in life is to raise a decent individual.

At this point, rejection sets in on the person without children. He or she wants time with the parent, who is trying to raise his or her child. The single person finds everything has deadlines, schedules, and certain times for being impromptu. It's irritating to the single because he or she never had to deal with so much detailed planning.

Over time, the single argues that he or she feels used, or way down on the bottom of the totem pole. Guess what? They are! Then, there's an unnatural feeling to receive attention from the parent. The single feels like he or she is only part of the parent's "schedule."

Many building blocks or natural progressions have been eliminated in this dating relationship. It's time alone together that builds intimacy, allows discovery of likes, dislikes, attitudes, and all the rest in order to become less selfish and more sacrificing.

The person without kids jumped from singleness to parenthood due to the position of the other person's life. The person with the child tries to become more "single," while the child suffers with that choice. In either case, *neither adult can experience the godly hierarchy of relationship as they tug and push against nature!*

Some people adapt to these situations. However, I believe it's few and far in between. There's too much imbalance to achieve success in a blended family, even though we may care deeply about the other person. When you hear, "we're just at different points in our lives," the meaning is clear. It's hard for a single to catch up with someone who's experienced everything including, the blessings and hardships of raising a child.

On the other hand, if both people bring children into a dating relationship, I don't know how they find mutual time together. Not only do they have the career calendar to contend with, but there are sports activities, music lessons, tutoring, schoolwork, and all the rest a parent has to juggle if life permits. How can the other parent become second or third on their totem pole? Guess what? They can't!

Summing up the situation, there's only one cure. That is, parents should commit to raising their kids with the assistance of the missing biological parent until their children leave the bird's nest. People may be shaking their heads, but is it better for multiple marriages or cohabitation situations to come and go, while the offspring watch all of the turmoil and confusion? We need to attend to the things committed to us and not worry about what's hiding in "greener pastures." We just don't know what we'll step into!

Nonetheless, hierarchal priorities remain in conflict when marriage occurs under the conditions described. Having biological parents overcome their differences through counseling might help save a family. I believe men should rise above the threat of expressing hurt and emotion in order to save what they're responsible for... *their families.*

79

# Chapter 8

## Respect, Honor and Submission

After understanding the basic concept of hierarchal priority, let's take a brief look at respect, honor, and submission. These virtues are a bridge, linking the first priority (God) to the second priority (man) in relationship with a woman. We will bridge the virtue of love that links God to a woman in relationship with a man in Chapter 20.

First, we must understand foundational truths about respect, honor and submission. Respect is developed and earned over time. Respect is established by giving unselfish attention to a person, accepting another's boundaries or similar character. Once respect flourishes, trust enters the picture. *Someone earns trust after they have gained respect.*

Honoring a person is accepting who they are because of their devotion, dedication, faithfulness, dependability, and so forth. Hence, many times we lose respect for someone because we thought we could trust them. Unfortunately, they weren't as honorable, or devoted, as we may have thought. They ended up *deceiving* us.

As we know, submission has an array of distorted interpretations. Many men may think it means having *dominance* over a woman as the "Commander In Chief," or being an authoritative ruler. Well, not really. Having *dominion* (the granted authority by God to rule) is what was given man, *not* dominance! Now, we need to tie all of this together.

We realize that respect, honor, and submission should have been rehearsed in a dating relationship. It's what helped consummate a marriage! For our example below, we'll assume it portrays a married couple who try to keep God their number one hierarchal priority.

A man's first need from his wife is *respect*. Disrespect arrives if she doesn't *honor* his position of dominion, or godly headship. Respect and honor tie to *submission*. Submission is evidence of a woman's *love* and *trust* in her husband's ability to lead the family because of his submission to God. Submission isn't a man telling his mate what to do, nor is it treating a woman like a slave. This is better known as *abuse!*

*A woman's submission is yielding to her godly husband's tie-breaking decision, resulting from unresolved conflict between them!* For example, if conflict arises between spouses on how to discipline their child, the man's responsibility is to evaluate both sides of the argument and determine a godly solution. If conflict doesn't exist over an issue, then submission, in this context, isn't utilized because of mutual agreement. Mutual agreement prevailed because each person *respected* and *honored* the other person's view!

Equally, a *man's submission is yielding to God's tie-breaking decision, from His word, resulting from confusion regarding conflict with his wife and the decision he is about to make.* Hence, if he and his wife disagree that spanking is or isn't appropriate, he must know God's viewpoint regarding discipline. If he finds that God condones such punishment, then his wife should submit to his final decision. His *dominion* (the granted authority by God to rule) is established. If he cannot find this action permitted by God, *he must respect, honor, and submit* to God's spiritual law.

It's difficult for a godly woman to submit to an ungodly man. He utilizes his own authoritative nature without any spiritual guidance. It's imperative for him to possess godly wisdom if he expects submission from his wife. If his wife is more spiritually in tune, she must follow what is most wise, even though he may try to convince her otherwise. This exemplifies the necessity of a personal relationship with God, and the importance of being "equally yoked" spiritually. It defines why roles and hierarchal priorities may get reversed in order to keep God's law a priority.

All in all, if a man is passive with God and doesn't respect, honor and submit to Him, most likely, a man will be passive in many types of relationships and not know how to properly respect, honor, or submit to anyone in authority. These three virtues are the foundation of our relational problems and are weaved throughout this writing.

### Becoming a godly Man
Maybe I should ask the question, "how does a man become a godly man?" In my teens and twenties, I believed I became "more of a man" after accomplishing some of my major goals. Making it through boot camp and the military, receiving top grades, graduating engineering school and making good money, are examples of this. Actually, it was becoming worldlier, not more of a man. I was preparing for the world ahead of me, but it had nothing to do with manhood.

I never realized the difference between godliness and manhood until I was thirty years of age. At that time, I accepted a *personal* relationship with Christ as my Lord and Savior. I *knew* who He was previously, but my experience was never personal with Him. Within days of my new relationship I remember saying, "*I feel like a man!*" I saw and felt the difference between me creating my own world, and becoming a *godly* man. *The only way a male can become a godly man is by humbling himself to someone of higher dominion than himself!*

Thank God He provides someone with more power and dominion than us! If God didn't provide His Son, men would have no one to submit to! This was an imperative part of God's perfect plan. Nonetheless, after finding this truth, I was angry with the world and how it led me to believe I had everything under control. It took years for my path to straighten, but it happened as I allowed the *greatest Man* of all time to work through me.

Are you a "self-made" worldly man, or are you allowing the power of God to work through you to create the man He envisions? Are you allowing Him to refine and define your masculinity? *A man cannot be referred to as a "gentleman" until he first becomes a godly man!*

Becoming godly requires humbling ourselves to our Creator and allowing Him to be the "potter" of our innate make-up. He creates gentlemen by removing the heavy burden of rejection, fear, anxiety and stress from us. Our world becomes a revolving door of respect, honor, and submission between Him and ourselves in singleness, and extends to our wives or future wives in marriage. Passivity is not allowed; only godly boldness and assertiveness, through masculinity, that God has granted us.

## Taking godly Action

My dad was a godly man. He assumed the role of husband and father by making sane, responsible, and sacrificial decisions. Life can't be lived successfully by being selfish or self-centered. Blood vessels scream when it is all about "me." There's no peace, sanity, tranquility or purpose. Even though my father feared God, he didn't pretend to be "holier than thou." He entertained a godly *lifestyle,* not an attitude.

The whole concept of Christianity is to imitate Christ's character. He was steeped in *wisdom* and full of *action*! My dad acquired these virtues because of life's turmoil. *That is what made him humble himself to God!* It wasn't the "going to church part" of this. Realizing he couldn't do it all on his own, he submitted to God and put Him first in hierarchal priority. By doing this, he had higher wisdom to lean on to help determine his actions from day to day. He also gained respect, honor and submission from his wife!

Christ's *actions* through teaching, healing, suffering and dying are what made Him great! His life was *all* action. Just as my dad submitted to God, *Christ submitted also in order to achieve His purpose!* Every task we have been assigned, large or small, from singleness to marriage, requires greater wisdom and power than ourselves to achieve.

Shortly after birth, my eyes were found crossed. My dad did everything possible to correct them. He even slapped me up side the head a few times... Well actually, after nine years and four surgeries, they were as straight as they were going to get!

He didn't stop at one or two surgeries, he continued until my eyes were as straight as possible! He didn't just sit there and pray while my eyes were unhealthy. He took action! By moving forward in action combined with prayer, the results came that he desired. I remember him telling me he had no insurance coverage on some of the surgeries.

Being a parent and developing a child for productivity in society is totally unselfish. Most men accepted their dutiful roles given to them many years ago in the family and work place. Today, it's shameful to hear about deadbeat dads. These dads don't take any responsibility for the chores God created for them to carry out in the family.

Imagine if Christ abandoned His purpose and role. The surgery needed on our hearts would've never been accomplished. He didn't just sit and pray that we'd be healed. He made a sane and responsible decision to suffer for His children's welfare. It was a totally unselfish act, so that His kids could be a useful part of His society. He stayed until the end and didn't stop at four lashes. He suffered until our relationship with Him could be as straight as possible! He deserves our respect, honor and submission for His sacrifice!

Marriage and parenthood are supposed to be blessings. Why then, are countless parents making insane and irresponsible decisions regarding their children's welfare? What's the reason for a parent's selfishness and abandonment of their roles before reaching the end? Why has the surgery been stopped when spouses are not straight relationally? Why are children left behind with emotional, spiritual, mental, and even physical bruises? Why don't parents carry spiritual insurance policies to help protect against divorce? Why has godly action dissipated?

### Becoming an action Dad
It came across my thoughts recently about the awesome responsibility a father has to his son or daughter in childhood, and especially in his or her adolescent years. I finally grasped the profound impact dads have on each gender in their adult life.

I realized that as a girl grows up, she needs protection, security and love from her dad. As a boy grows up, he seeks respect and honor for who he is at that moment in time, and who he wants to become in the future. A boy looks for approval and support from his father. I think most of us are in agreement with these statements so far.

Within moments, I recognized what each gender seeks in a life-long relationship. A woman needs protection, security and *love* from her husband! A man needs *respect*, *honor* and approval of who he is at that moment in time and who he wants to become in the future! The husband seeks support from his wife. *"However, each one of you must also love his wife as he loves himself, and the wife must respect her husband"* (Eph 5:33).

An assumption regarding fathers can be made from what's been stated. That is, *it's imperative for dad to be selfless and unselfish in raising his children, in order that the child will know what to expect and receive in a marriage from his or her spouse!* Dad is an integral part in the development of his children, just like God, Our Heavenly Father, has an integral part in developing His children of both genders!

Maybe scores of relationships end up in the pits because earthly fathers are failing to assist in the development of their children. Since dad's children, of either gender, have a sour image of him, they also have the same sour image of their Heavenly Father. Thus, the children aren't allowing God to develop them! Maybe dad didn't exhibit love or respect to his son. Dad judged or talked down to his daughter making her feel insecure, unloved, and without a strong sense of protection. His problems were perhaps deep enough to invade his precious daughter's innocence.

Now, we have two genders of children leaving home looking for love. What will they end up with? They'll find another person who has no idea of what true relationship means. A young woman will crave security, love and protection as she tries to control her man to get it. She may be demanding because of the hurt she experienced. A young man may get angry because he doesn't receive the respect, acceptance or support he needs from his wife to get to where he wants to be in the future. It all stems from the negligence of the father.

*The healthiest way for a child to enter matrimony is having a father actively involved in the child's life to provide the assets each gender needs.* If a child never receives these virtues from dad, it will be a struggle to get through life successfully regarding any relationship, including one with God. Respect and submission to authority will be voided.

If you're a husband and/or father, it's time to get off the couch, put food on the table, and provide security, love and protection that your wife and daughter seek in their worlds. It's time to stop ridiculing your son for not being perfect and respect his desires for the future. Show you're a person with a heart and leave selfishness and self-centeredness behind. More importantly, people other than yourself are waiting for you to do what's required to bring unity in the family! It is *your* responsibility.

Macho personas are heavy masks to carry. Start showing love through *action.* Stop being a "best buddy" to your son or daughter. By doing this, it displays weakness, and actually looks as if you are seeking acceptance from a child needing your firm love! It's time to realize other people are counting on you! Become conscious that you're destroying lives under your roof. Change the crowd you hang with, your old habits, or whatever you are involved with, and get some help! It's time to become an action dad!

Why are some men scared to get help? I believe it's three-fold. First, they believe nothing was their fault. Everyone feels like that! But, they may have been handed a bad deck of cards initially and don't realize the problem. Secondly, they really don't know how to communicate and think it is girly stuff. Finally, there is so much deep pain involved, it's difficult to approach. They wrongly believe their authority figure persona would be endangered if they got advice from someone who might bring insight to their soul.

*Masculinity isn't being tough, in charge, or authoritative. Masculinity means being men of our word, men who provide, protect and love unconditionally. Masculinity is a call to stand up in the best interests of our families. It admits our need for a woman to help shape our relational abilities. There may be times masculinity sheds a tear because the load is too heavy, or it may require great humbleness. Masculinity fights for what is right, with passion only possessed and understood from deep within. Masculinity is called upon to test our ability to make decisions standing on our feet. Masculinity is submitting to God and His ways. Masculinity is an awesome virtue with which to be blessed.*

Any man who believes that masculinity is defined by a deep voice, large biceps, tough nature, big tattoos or bad language is incorrect. With all due respect, these traits indicate a hurt little boy who needs help. Maybe dad didn't treat us properly, and it's showing up more than we know. If we saw ourselves as others do, we may not like what we see.

I know what it's like to carry hurt. I know my hurt injured family and friends. It's ok to admit assistance is needed to heal our innocence. If we get assistance, we have to be open and honest. As time progresses, we'll discover trust in a person who'll actually listen without judgment. No one is perfect; we're all short of a "happy meal!" It's called being human. God forbid those who judge our humanity because they're in deep denial!

# Chapter 9

## Feminine Men, Masculine Women

Respect, honor, submission, godliness, masculinity, and femininity have all been uniquely interwoven to this point. When these traits are prioritized and displayed properly, our individuality can be expressed more confidently. In order for us to operate smoothly within our gender, we need to understand our innate structures from a new perspective.

Do you think it's acceptable for some men to be more feminine or for some women to be more masculine? Even though many men are raised to be "tough" and some women as "submissive," it can negate the fact that some females may exhibit more masculinity than femininity, or males more femininity than masculinity. Could the creation of Adam have anything to do with all of this?

When Adam was created, there wasn't any companion available for him. So, one day God put him into a deep sleep, removed one of his ribs and created a woman. No longer was man to be alone. So, for the moment, we all need to be at "ground zero" and assume this is true. It will help me explain a pretty dynamic reality.

We know that masculinity holds the virtues of hunter, pursuer, provider, and protector. Because Adam was the first man on earth made in God's image, he needed these devices to have purpose and to be able to survive on his own. He was created to hunt for food and provide for his stomach. He pursued his work, and was to protect his future mate from being deceived.

We know that femininity holds the virtues of nurturing, caring, being emotional, mothering, and so forth. Hence, if woman was created from man's rib that means *man already carried feminine traits within him! He was initially equipped with emotion, nurturing, and other feminine traits before woman was formed.* At the same time, a woman holds masculine traits because she is directly from Adam's bones!

I believe when "the surgery" was performed on man, certain degrees of *his* feminine part were divinely left within him. At the same instance, woman inherited a portion of his masculine side. This delicate, intricate and omnipotent design is the basis for mutual attraction of the opposite sex. The amount of masculinity and femininity in every person may vary. It allows a man and woman to reunite in order to become "one flesh" in marriage. Now, man would be *complete* once again like he was before "the surgery."

Being *complete* is different than being *whole.* Being whole is having contentment, peace and solitude within one's self. There is a lack of selfish pride, greed, envy, and other ungodly traits. It is the result of having dealt with many ill emotions.

Being complete is having the privilege to share our wholeness with another whole person. It allows us to experience an abundant life. This type of life would reflect love, peace, joy, solitude, kindness, boldness, assertiveness, passion, abundance and prosperity, all driven by masculinity and femininity.

Being whole allows us to reap a harvest that includes obtaining our heart's desire. In most cases, a person's heart's desire is acceptance, honor, love and respect from a significant other. Careers, money and possessions would be reaped, and would be seen as a *blessing,* instead of something we are entitled to. This is why Christ said, *"But seek first His kingdom and His righteousness, and all these things will be given to you as well"* (Mat 6:33).

Once a man finds his "missing rib," there's no need to suppress or hide his emotions. Emotion isn't weakness; *it's an avenue to establish strength as wholeness is being sought.* It's human to cry and talk about feelings, not sissy, as some may think. A woman can see inside a man because that's where she came from! She has inner strength, to support him, from the masculine part residing in her. Thus, a man has been awarded an *emotional helpmate!*

A woman innately seeks leadership and a strong hand that is gentle. She does not always want a "tough" guy. She wants to feel safe with a man. Gentlemen, we must realize that our wives, or future wives, are part of our own flesh. *We are seeing our insides... outside of us!* She is there to make us complete *"as it was in the beginning."*

## Gender Equilibrium

When I mentioned that the amount of masculinity and femininity in every person may vary, it's important to consider gender equilibrium. Some may think it's the struggle to "balance" our innate qualities with the opposite sex. Others may think it is the ability to "do it all," or many may believe it's the *act* of being masculine or feminine.

We've somehow attained the idea that men are supposed to be completely masculine and women absolutely feminine. Actually, I don't think it works this way. It's impossible to be entirely one trait or another. We aren't talking about being a male or female, but rather it's about being masculine or feminine.

When a man pursues to seek his "missing rib," *gender equilibrium,* or *balance*, needs to exist between each other's masculine and feminine sides in the relationship.

For example, if a masculine man marries a more masculine than feminine woman, there may be struggle for control, power and position. The relationship would revolve around who "wore the pants." If a masculine man marries a more feminine woman, there's more room for conversation, compliments and intimacies. Thus, they're comfortable in their positions and can rely on each other when needed.

Conversely, if a more feminine than masculine man marries a feminine woman, they may cry on each other's shoulder! There's no headship. But, if a more feminine male marries a more masculine female, gender equilibrium returns. Power struggles and so forth wouldn't be an issue because the couple would naturally compliment one another.

When speaking of a masculine woman, I don't mean the way she walks or talks at this point. I am referring to her ambitions, drive, and desires. Is she a hunter, protector or provider? When I speak of a feminine man, I don't mean the way he walks or talks. I am speaking of the emotions he exhibits or the nurturing he is able to give.

This explains why every man cannot marry just any "rib!" Every man and woman has a different level of masculinity and femininity within themselves. Billions of dollars are spent to determine personalities, temperaments, astrological compatibilities, genetic structure, likes, dislikes, and childbirth order to "solve" our relational inabilities. We actually need the intricate measurement of masculinity and femininity within us to be studied!

Five thousand questions of our likes, dislikes, habits, religious beliefs and all the rest will not determine life long compatibility! Any two people can agree or disagree on such things as religion, smoking and drinking habits, or where they prefer to live. What counts is how people handle themselves in good times and bad, how they act or react in desperate situations, or how they allow another to contribute what's most natural to them. *Ensuring that gender equilibrium exists will assist in providing life long compatibility!*

Thus, if a man taps into his feminine side or a woman taps into her masculine side, they may be better balanced, and possess a higher understanding of the opposite sex. These men and women usually possess a better *appreciation* for the other gender. If this occurs, they experience deeper compassion and respect for their mate. It allows love and intimacy to grow. They will have a little bit more to offer each other in good times or bad, and they will inherit a deeper bond.

### Acting it Out
Aren't we told that if a man sheds a tear in front of a woman, it shows signs of weakness rather than strength? Men aren't supposed to cry or show this type of emotion. Men are tough! Showing their feminine side would be acting as sissy or weak. Yet, a woman would appreciate this part of a man.

Consequently, negative emotions build up in males because they won't release them naturally. Conversation, crying, or counseling just isn't their bag. A man's pent up emotional energy usually converts to anger, while the pressures of not releasing his feelings can be explosive.

Since many men are raised one-sided, they typically

believe that masculinity equates to "toughness." Due to their "toughness," they're unable to identify with a woman's *innate* emotional side. Her natural emotions may include the general concern over the well-being of her husband and children, which are connected to her nurturing and care-giving capabilities. She wants to keep her family from harm. It would devastate her if any of her loved ones were injured or hurt. Additionally, a woman's menstrual cycle creates natural hormonal changes resulting in emotions that she may be unable to control.

Conversely, if a woman *"acts out"* her emotions to control a man or to attain sympathy to win her way, these *unnatural* emotions may be recognized by a man and fuel his resentment towards her. It's hard for him to become sympathetic or compassionate in these situations, even though a woman may crave some attention to sooth her insecurity.

Then, there are times when a woman says, "I also have a feminine side." What does she mean? Perhaps she's admitting to her conscious effort to *act* masculine. This now refers to the way she walks, talks, or expresses herself. It may be an avenue to display her anger towards men. Most men won't approach these types of women. Instantly, a man's toughness or walls may shoot up. A woman's chance of meeting a good man then lessens, and these men might become more passive in approaching *other* women. If a woman used her innate feminine qualities, she would notice improved health in mind, body, spirit, and relationships.

If a woman acts out anything that depletes her femininity, her life becomes more complicated and stressful. God never intended for women to act out, or attempt to accomplish what men are geared to do. Perhaps some women would feel inadequate if they didn't try to fulfill this ridiculous effort. Nature tells her she is more nurturing, but she's battling with what's programmed on her "hard drive." Thus, in a relationship, she doesn't understand why her mate feels *worthless, unappreciated, or unneeded.* She was raised one-sided, and may not understand the values or purpose of a man.

For centuries, we have been led astray regarding the perceptions of masculinity and femininity. Currently, the confusion is rampant and hurting scores of individuals. It becomes a lot more confusing when money is involved. In the next chapter, we will approach the complicated issue of money that men and women face on a daily basis.

# Chapter 10

# The Complicated Money Game

My masculine side has always wanted to protect and provide for "my girl." On the other hand, I see many women seeking opportunities in the working world, and yet desire to be pampered by a man monetarily. Some men cannot unleash this perplexity. Now, money becomes an issue. Please be patient for a moment as I try to unravel this!

Take Ken and Beth for example. Beth makes a good living, and understands that Ken's desire is to *provide* while her desire is for *security*. So, she may switch roles from "provider" to "deserving recipient" in order to have it all. However, *we can't have it all!*

Ken battled with this dilemma before his first or second date with Beth. Nonetheless, he wants to treat her appropriately. He set his financial boundaries before going out, but he may exceed his limits in order to display selflessness and to make a good impression. The issue here is Ken's fear and insecurity of losing Beth, even though she was never his!

Nonetheless, he subconsciously questions Beth's motive. Is she being sincere or are her feelings of rejection, acquired from other men, being taken out on Ken through very pretty eyes for a night of bliss?

Ken can handle the fact that there's a fifty-fifty chance for him to see Beth again. He felt obligated to spend his money in good faith because of his need to provide. The problem Ken faces is that he can't separate the innate pressure to provide from the pressure of trying to impress a woman because of his pride. Ken ends up thinking, "I just spent tons of money on Beth who makes more than I do. She might not want to see me again, but her entertainment is my debt! When do equal rights come into play?"

Once securing a learning curve, Ken restrains monetarily with new acquaintances. Now, his goal is to seek a woman's motive before reaching into his pocket. If a woman encounters Ken, who has now gained wisdom regarding motives, she may think he's a tightwad! She might feel he hasn't spent enough money on her, and she looks elsewhere. Ken concludes that money was her only concern to win him the date in the first place.

Consequently, men or women repress anger after being used financially. In Ken's case, he had the privilege of Beth's company, but he felt used. In order to avoid this feeling on subsequent dates with other women, Ken's approach may come across harsher. Now he gets rejected more, and scares women away because of his bitterness.

### Women who Pay

What about women offering to pay their fair share on a first or second date? They may be sincere, but this can push a guy's button to *provide*. Or, she may want to pay because of no interest in her date! She doesn't want him to feel obligated, but may be too embarrassed to tell him why. He'd love to go "Dutch," but his pride might confirm that she wouldn't want to see him again by suggesting it. His need to provide persists, however, because he envisions another meeting. On the other hand, he'll be upset if he does pay without a subsequent date. This might be referred to as a "man's ego" when, by design, *it's his nature to provide*. Frustration builds because he is caught in the middle and can't help how he's wired... again.

Once a relationship is established, many women do flip the tab. They're sincerely generous. Sadly, *they* may be taken advantage of financially because of their choice in a man. He ends up on the sofa not working! He chose to lay out all his money in the beginning to make an impression. Additionally, some lies he told start to surface. She not only pays for dinner, but she also pays an emotional price because of his idleness.

Her mistakes are realized and it's hard to turn back. Her emotional investment pursues hope for him to play his part. This constantly occurs in dating, yet marriages still transpire. Months or years down the road a divorce surfaces because a husband never held a job. Well, if he didn't hold one while dating, why would he have one in marriage?

Let's realize a basic reality. *"What you see is what you get and what you got is what you saw!"* People usually don't change. We hope for it, but it mostly remains only a hope. Why is that? You've got it! Internal conflicts are eating away without resolve.

## How much money is Enough?
Chitchat reveals that some women are getting tired of the corporate rat race. Some married women want to go back to being homemakers, and single women wish they had a home to go to! However, both married and single women are used to certain lifestyles. If a married woman quits working now, her lifestyle may become less affluent. This is hard to accept along with potentially seeing her husband work another job. Now, he may never be home.

Holy confusion! He realizes the difficulty of life. He

steps out trying to become a multimillionaire and attempts every get rich quick scheme there is. These schemes don't work, and he goes into deeper debt. He wants to throw in the towel and run.

I knew several good men, never married, between the ages of thirty-eight and forty-eight. They were successful and good-looking, but never felt money was plentiful. In one case, a friend made over $10,000.00 per month! I couldn't believe he insisted it wasn't enough. His fear of insufficiency came from dating experiences in the early 1990's. In the 21st century, scores of women refuse to date a guy who makes less than six figures!

Then we hear about financially successful career women who say that men are *intimidated* by their achievements. Actually, a much deeper emotion is often felt called *sorrow*. A man realizes his chance of experiencing femininity may be limited. He knows this woman's hierarchal priorities aren't geared for creating a *successful* family life.

Thus, family life would be a never-ending battle. He might enjoy her financial freedom and support her success, but this is his insecure side talking because he doesn't measure up financially. Sooner or later he'll feel defeated because it's his innate desire to provide. Furthermore, her schedule does not always allow for either of their needs to be fulfilled. The end result is his passivity and her control.

Both genders are confused when it comes to monetary outlay. It's actually tied to a fear of being hurt from rejection. If money is forked out, either party wants to see their investment grow. If mutual attraction doesn't exist, communication often fails or someone feels used. Then after enough repetition of this cycle, anger riles, roles self-destruct, and respect is lost for the next girl or guy.

This often leads to prenuptial agreements forced on either gender before marriage. In some cases, it's advisable if a lot of money is involved. However, in today's world, many people with little money are doing it, perhaps because of a divorce they've experienced. This actually translates to a lack of *trust* after rejection in a previous marriage. I don't believe marriage would be worth consummating at this point because the innate functions and dignity of a person can be easily damaged.

## Having it Better

We know how parents love their children and want the best for them. They want them *"to have it better"* than they did. What does this entail?

I see all the materialism surrounding our communities and wonder, "how much better could their kids have it anyway?" The struggle to keep up with material gain is painful and worthless. We look forward to something and once we get it, the thrill is gone and it's time for something new. It's *unfulfilling!* Our struggle is internal once again.

Parents may go broke trying to fund their child's college fund or retirement account, instead of their own. Some parents strive to provide luxuries for their child which makes them idle in society. A *worthy* investment would be to provide their child with love, security, support, approval, one on one time with dad, and most of all, discipline. Surely, if they received all of this, they would definitely *"have it much better than their parents did."*

How much money is enough? There is never enough; we'll never fill our spiritual void. It provides stress and grief,

103

and we'll acquire a lackluster life by chasing it. On the other hand, how much love is enough? There is never enough; we will crave it until the afterlife! The nice thing is that love is free to give and free to take. It provides contentment, joy, happiness and peace!

# Chapter 11

## Financial Stress & Irresponsibility

A man is required by God to provide for his family in the best possible way. If he or his wife spends money past their affordability level, they compress valid feelings of unneeded pressure. We know anger stems from this, and emotions can explode from financial stress at any moment. What takes the first hit? Correct... our marriage or the opportunity to be married. Money problems continue with or without a mate.

In my younger years, I believed it was my responsibility to provide. Things changed, and I've tried to grasp the concept of countless working mothers. For some reason it just doesn't seem right. As I've become more financially enabled, I look at a prospective mate's financial condition from the outside. If she is upside down financially, for the wrong reasons, she's no longer a prospect.

This is another reason it may take longer to find a mate. Why get involved with someone who will help bring us down financially when we fought so hard to stay afloat? Many people would call something like this being "too picky." No, it's being *prudent*.

Personal spiritual issues increase debt on family credit cards and home equity loans. Envy, competition, greed, divorce, and the ill emotion of what others think we can afford are on the list. When I was a banker, I noticed people arrived having these ridiculous rivalries with neighbors, spouses, girlfriends, boyfriends and themselves.

105

We all know prosperity reigns in the United States. It's quite ironic because personal debt has hit the trillion-dollar mark! That doesn't include mortgages. Then we hear how most retirees rely on social security for retirement. Concurrently, we play the lottery to solve our problems. Sadly, many people who win these jackpots usually end up broke. Why is that? Once again, it's due to internal conflicts and unresolved spiritual issues.

When it comes to a vehicle, we might lease it to avoid a large down payment, and for a lower monthly payment. As a result, we never own it, as money is thrown into the wind. Others may envy us and rush out to keep up with our luxury. Within moments of their envy, their credit is stretched to help push their financial status onto shakier ground. They have now extended themselves into the realm of financial stress and irresponsibility.

Once retirement approaches, working may have to continue because no savings was established in our youth. We shouldn't worry though; we looked good behind the wheel for many years. No one on the planet really cared about what we drove except a pretentious date. Nonetheless, every month we had the pressure to try and make the payments in order to drive a brand new car or truck every two or three years!

We hardly own homes anymore. It's all about size. How big can my house get in order to impress parents, siblings, or people from the street? I can only afford to spend $180,000.00 on a house, but if I get an interest only loan, I can afford a $300,000.00 house!

This is a great opportunity to go broke. If we only pay interest and the principle never goes down, and the interest rates go up, we are in what they call foreclosure! There are thousands of foreclosures in the Atlanta area every month because of this way of thinking. How many are coast to coast? Bankruptcies are out of control. But! We are prosperous!

The whole point of mentioning these facts is that a family can't survive under these pressures! When people realize that others cannot afford what they have, not own what they have, and know it's mostly paper transactions that gives them what they have, then maybe people can be happy with what they do have. Remember the saying, "It isn't having what you want, its wanting what you have?"

Is the 6,000 square foot house or SUV that guzzles our lunch money at a stoplight more important than having a good meal? Why are families forfeiting relationships for materialism? Why are *things* more precious than human affection and love? How come children have to suffer immensely over the greediness of a parent? Why do we believe the lies, experience them first hand and end up in the pits, only to start all over again?

Have we ever considered how prosperous this country would truly be if divorce rates were less than 20%? When we go into the second, third or fourth marriage with monetary layouts, people can go broke financially, emotionally, mentally, and spiritually. Yet, people paying out alimony and child support somehow live in big homes and drive big cars. So, in order to get by, we have to rely on the credit card and home equities!

If families stayed together with the amount of money being made out there today, homes would be paid off, moms could stay at home, the retirement account would look pretty good, and Christmas would probably be a lot less stressful.

However, many people have forgotten that spiritual laws govern true prosperity!

If we're meant to be millionaires... we'll certainly be millionaires and the money will last when God ordains it. Many have hoped, or have been taught, that tithing would make them rich! Well, not really. When a person tithes, God promises to meet their *needs*; you know... food, clothing and shelter. Reaching beyond our needs because of greed may result in grief, ruin, anxiety, fear, bankruptcy, and a stressful retirement. Is it really worth it?

## Your house or Mine?

Even though men are innately designed to be providers, some feel defeated in supplying these basic needs, as outlined above. Many times subtle uneasiness or stress is created in a dating relationship because of what another person may own. Let's use the example of home ownership.

We're all aware that we need a roof over our heads. Thank God, most of us have one! Nonetheless, both a man and a woman may have purchased their own house, or a person of either gender owns a house, and the other doesn't. If someone is financially capable to buy a house, it's a wise and prudent financial decision. Some people just don't want the responsibility of home ownership for one reason or another.

However, when a couple begins dating, they check out each other's abode. If a man owns a house and the woman doesn't, the man feels adequate and wants to provide her this "luxury." She's likely to be excited, hoping she would be under his roof one day. It is part of the security she seeks.

On the other hand, if a woman owns a house and the man doesn't, he may experience a feeling of inadequacy.

Because of her possession, it may trigger a sense of "power or control" she has over him. It negates his feeling to provide, or he might feel he can't live up to her "expectant" lifestyle.

Some may feel he is insecure. Actually, we're dealing with *innate desires* again, *not emotional insecurity.* Most likely, a woman is unaware of this fine line between being "wired a certain way," and a man's insecurities. He may feel discouraged with not being able to exercise his innate aspirations, especially when it's associated with *providing.* A man wants to *give* to show his love. If a woman already has everything, or has experienced a lot of life's pleasures, he feels no reason to give.

Nevertheless, if both parties own a house, it makes things much harder to compromise. The couple has to come to an agreement whether one of the houses should be rented, sold, or if they should live in *"your house or mine."* If it comes down to the latter, it makes either gender feel they must submit to the lifestyle of the other person as they "rule the roost."

If financial conditions warrant, it would be best if both parties owning a home sold them and selected a new house *together.* It helps unite "two fleshes" as "one." Of course, there may be the issue of school districts, how big a house needs to be due to a home-based business, or the number of combined kids, etc. It goes on and on. Wasn't it much easier when people got married, and remained married, under one roof?

The independence of both genders has perhaps reached levels that interfere with relationship processing in a profound and cruel manner. There is a definite clash of masculine and feminine objectives. Many obstacles need to be overcome, that never needed this much serious consideration before. It's difficult to regroup and make the necessary adjustments. Nonetheless, *the only adjustment that needs to be made is to allow masculinity and femininity to "rule the roost!"*

# Chapter 12

## Getting Past Attitude & Entitlement

For over thirty years, I have sought life-long companionship by either trying too hard or not trying hard enough. At times, I've totally thrown in the towel, and hoped the old adage of not looking for someone would make them magically appear!

However, two prevalent issues seem to inhibit a man's pursuit and forward progression in meeting the opposite sex. Namely, they are getting past the *attitudes* and *entitlements* that some women exhibit in their behavior towards others. Unfortunately, numerous potential relationships are unlikely to be established because of these factors.

In reference to a woman, I will define *attitude* as the way she exhibits her personality. *Entitlement* is what she feels she deserves from another person because of her looks, figure, sex appeal or spoiled nature. Remember, *I'm only speaking about forward progression in getting to know someone.* I am not speaking about being in a relationship that is going forward.

What's the first thing a man notices about a woman? Yep, her overall look and sex appeal. Within nanoseconds, he notices her attitude. If her nose is white with cloud dust, he concludes she is "stuck up." She believes her physical beauty outweighs life itself. Then, within microseconds, the guy concludes her entitlement isn't worth his sincerity.

Now, he chooses to become someone he's not. He figures, a woman won't accept him if he were himself anyway.

So, he tries to determine what she wants in order to be accepted by her. This is done to "win" her. He attempts everything under the sun to get a date. If he does win her, he has to maintain his false persona. If he doesn't win her, he'll become more frustrated trying to figure out what *any* woman wants.

If a girl seems unapproachable or hard to please, and she feels she's too good for someone, not only does a man wear a mask, but he's most likely lost respect for her. He concludes her entitlement she seeks says, "Because I'm so gorgeous, I can only be seen in a new Corvette or BMW convertible. I'm way too good looking to be seen in a VW Rabbit." No, I don't drive a VW! Nonetheless, this basically describes the attitude/entitlement combo this type of woman exhibits.

If a man chose to try and communicate with this type of woman, it's because he is attracted to her and feels he might be able to "unlock her combination." If he was able to succeed, the embarrassment he faced was worth the risk. Nonetheless, if he doesn't succeed, he may still experience disappointment, and could still suppress emotions because of feeling rejected by her attitude and/or entitlement.

In most cases, a man's initial thought was *not* to get her into bed! He had a healthy attitude that was devoured little by little, due to the arrogance of this girl's attitude. All he sought was the *pleasure* of speaking to a woman that he thought was pretty. Maybe, with any luck, he would find the guts to ask her out and she would accept.

In reference to a man, we will define *attitude* as the way he exhibits his personality. Usually, a macho, cool or funny personality is played out. This is to impress a girl so he isn't rejected. He can fly from macho to funny in a heartbeat, back to macho, and invent some personalities in between it all. These guys become the strongman, rugged guy, Mr. Sentimental, or whatever they think the girl is looking for. They're trying to find a woman's "happy side." Once it's discovered, they lock into that position and "playact."

His *entitlement* states that he deserves the girl after all his work to impress her, *or* if he spent money on her, he needs to recoup it somehow. She has had enough of his stunts and can't wait to move on because she has witnessed his motive to capture her. However, many times with enough insistence, a date will come about.

We all need to get past attitude and entitlement. It's wasted energy and there's no substance on which to build a relationship. One might feel that I'm defining teenagers in relationships. Playing it out in our minds, it's probably true. However, it continues at any age with more "adult style and fashion." There's a difference, however; the dollar bills attached get bigger!

Men with money often think they have the answers to relationship. They feel entitled to sex because of a dollar bill. Several self-made, wealthy men are not like this. They want an old-fashioned woman, and hence, have remained single. Nonetheless, many women don't seem to get it. There are those who seem to love sloppy, abusive and selfish guys for some reason. They end up married, and end up divorced.

### Results of pester Power

Things our parents told us, did for us, required from us, handed to us, or allowed us to do without guidance, helped create our attitude and entitlement. Plenty of kids today lay down the rules for the parents and the parents oblige. It's called *"pester power."*

Let's say Jane becomes of driving age. She's excited to get her license. She passes her test. Now she wants a car. If she rebelled enough using "pester power" to get what she wanted while growing up, she'll do it again and get her car. It's great that mom and dad wish to help her out to get things rolling (no pun intended!), but they start her out with a new sports car edging toward the thirty thousand dollar mark. She's only sixteen!

Even though mom and dad may have neglected Jane growing up, the car proves their love to her. No values or responsibility are taught or learned. Things are handed over to hush the pestering. Parents have no control because they never disciplined their offspring from birth. Consequently, worthy relationships that Jane experiences could be very frail. Can't blame Jane for her attitude and entitlement being more powerful than her character!

Jane meets a guy and is clingy with him. Her attitude seems fine, but getting to know her, he discovers his money is disappearing at an exponential rate. He realizes that Jane is taking whatever she can get. She isn't stealing behind his back. She does it right under his nose! He's focused on how cute she is in the beginning, and believes it's natural to spend money on her. Society has always impressed on a man's mind that spending money on a girl is the proper etiquette to "open the door" to a relationship. *"No money... no honey!"*

After a few dates, he decides that there is too much pressure keeping up with her material wants. She drives off in a brand new sports car that her loving parents *gave* her. She never respected his money or hard work. To her, it's a foreign concept. The only way she would respect a man is if he did fulfill all of her material wants. Unfortunately, submissiveness in marriage could never be her virtue.

Going a little deeper, this young man is actually in direct competition with Jane's parents financially. The guy has no chance! He isn't educated or established yet. He'd feel "obligated" to fork out sums of money just to remain friends with this type of girl. Of course, there are some parents who would never allow such a "poor boy" to date their daughter anyway.

Now, he might experience anger and/or rejection. Plus, he may have childhood issues beneath it all. He was trying to be nice and meet a girl he was attracted to. Jane seemed fine up front, but, if he continues meeting girls like Jane, it can impact the respect he *should* have for other women. However, Jane continues to hunt for a wealthy man.

Jane's parents are to blame in this whole mess for not taking responsibility to raise a responsible individual. They've neglected and spoiled not only their daughter, but may have hindered other people, with a genuine heart, from entering Jane's life.

We understand Jane has a new car with payments and upkeep. Being so young, her parents probably fund the vehicle. Then, because mom and dad kept Jane quiet and proved their "love," they afforded her a car they couldn't afford! Most likely, Jane's parents will continue supporting her even if she's able to afford her own life.

Jane's parents soon reap a whirlwind of torments for spoiling her. Things like arguments over money issues and bankruptcy crop up, mostly because Jane's car costs too much to support. Dad becomes belligerent and doesn't get home on time to avoid watching the problems get bigger, until finally, the inevitable separation occurs.

## When a parent steps Up

I wanted a snowmobile when I was fourteen. My uncle had two of them and my cousin could ride whenever he wanted. So, one Christmas I laid a freeway of hints for my dad about having one. Finally, as I was staring out the window one snowy morning, he said, "I can't afford a snowmobile. If you want one, you will have to earn it."

It was heartbreaking for both my dad and me at that moment. However, I started saving money from my paper route, keeping score at the bowling alley, and pumping gas at his service station. In one year, I saved $500.00 in cash, and bought one of my uncle's snowmobiles! That's when I learned about money, and how difficult it was to save.

That one lesson has stuck with me. I maintain things entrusted to me because it's hard work to attain. If everything were given to me, it wouldn't be appreciated and I'd expect others to provide "my toys." Thankfully, my parents didn't feel *"less than"* by saying, *"no"* to me for something I did want. Thus, I don't need as many *things* because of the amount of work and upkeep required. I have more appreciation for *stuff*.

There were times I wanted to "disown" my parents for being so "non-giving." That was my selfish nature coming to surface, not theirs. They had seven kids! My attitude needed weaning from me! That was my parents' responsibility to achieve, not mine, while I lived under their roof. They were teaching us how to survive in a world as young men and women with character. Many times they surprised us with something that brought tears to our eyes. They went straight for our hearts!

Changing gears a bit, I'm sure many have heard about

the new popular gift received by teenage girls graduating high school. Cars and watches are losing ground to the latest present: breast implants! Why do parents allow such a thing before nature has completed its course? The most fashionable reason I hear is, "Whatever *keeps* her happy!"

The word "keeps," in other words, eliminates pestering. Hence, the parent will work another part time job, give loans, or just pay for the surgery, all for the girl's "happiness." They never tried approaching the "heartbreak moment," which hurts for a short time, to help instill a sense of responsibility into the teenager. The parents don't teach patience or even allow God a chance to finish developing the girl before they interfere!

Pestering didn't start overnight. It started way back in a child's developmental years, as rebellion, perhaps because the parents separated, divorced, or were too scared to discipline their children. Children need parents to help them understand what is or isn't acceptable.

It is tiresome to hear about small children who are out of control from birth. They are often medically diagnosed with a brain problem, chemical imbalance or A.D.D. A small percentage may have a medical problem. However, the remainders only need a hand of correction on their behind where God placed extra padding, especially if it's a boy!

Spanking isn't evil. It's what rearranges a kid's chemical imbalance so their brain won't forget! If this form of discipline is accomplished before attending school, teachers won't have to waste valuable classroom hours correcting misbehavior. Tantrums in the grocery store might be avoided! Mom and dad need to step up to the plate and remember the saying, *"this will hurt me more than it's going to hurt you!"*

After I was spanked once, my dad's hand was recalled. Thereafter, I only needed a stern look! This is how it seems to work, folks. Sadly, dads often aren't around, or perhaps mom is against godly discipline. Yep, *A.D.D.--A*bsent *D*ads & *D*iscipline. Is it coincidence that this "illness" became rampant alongside divorce? Drug companies feast on our despair!

# Chapter 13

## Through a Good Man's Eye

Discipline is the magic to create a good man or woman. Disciplined people aren't into playing games on the dating field, nor are they into secular power trips. A good man craves an unpretentious woman for his future wife. Nevertheless, I've detected competition regarding looks, career, or intelligence with a date. She may struggle to be equal or try to outrank me, perhaps in an effort to be accepted.

Usually, men don't consider the worldly achievements of a woman on their list of needs. The topic of career can be scary. Sometimes, her emotion, linked to her work, has him wonder if he'll ever receive as much. If this isn't the case, he may pretend to show interest in the beginning and hopes the topic fades. In his mind, he's picturing a supportive girlfriend or prospective wife who loves him as much as she articulates the "love of her job."

Whatever the case, I carry an extreme burden and sadness for some women. Many have been taught that their worldly achievements are more important than their presence in the home, or that the world will crumble without them. Well, the world *is* crumbling without them, by them *not* being in the home! Here's what these women might see "through a good man's eye:"

*They'd witness befuddled women in business settings trying to stay up with corporate pressures and responsibilities. This is accompanied by loneliness, pain, sorrow, and stress. They'd see women sitting behind large desks with paper piled sky high and out of control. In this setting, their wedding rings would lack luster and the shine they once had, even though the diamond is two carats large!*

*From afar, these women might feel a husband's pain of loneliness, and the lack of attention he and the children receive as a wife fearlessly works overtime. They'd feel a devastating blow to her family because her energy to nurture has been depleted. They'd see she's blinded from the truth, knowing it's not natural for her to be away from home so long. They may witness her feeling "less than" to the world if she was home with her kids. She feels smarter and stronger than squandering her time with such trivial matters.*

*They would see pregnant women, in the working world, proving how strong they are and that they can balance the load. These women look confident, serious, professional and precise. But, for some reason, it doesn't appear the way they may think.*

*They'd see how the world destroys the best part of a woman's youth. They'd witness how a woman's looks define her femininity. Then, one day, a single woman might desire a family, but she's too old, or worn out. Her innate desire churns to have a child. Men aren't available, but the sperm banks or adoption centers are.*

*They would view a deadbeat dad who doesn't care about his child's welfare, as his child struggles to receive love and acceptance. They would see a devastated woman left behind for another, causing her to struggle financially without any of his assistance.*

*These women would also see some women on the streets helping to protect our communities. At the same time, they'd see her uniform used as a barrier to help protect her from physical harm. The uniform represents her power and strength. It's foolish to think her physical strength would ever exceed that of a wild man. Respect for the uniform, if one has any respect at all, is her only hope.*

*On the other hand, these women would see sincere, feminine ladies, who are helpless in a world pushing them off to the side because they are too old-fashioned. These women don't carry the brut strength and politically correct qualities that will make them "fit" into society. Even though they are what a woman should be, they remain alone because of their unwillingness to conform to modern day practices.*

It's difficult for true femininity to present itself well in a man's world, no matter what numbers of women are in it. God created man to toil the earth and built him to deal with this task, with the support of a wife. Even though most Americans believe in God, they don't seem to heed to basic truth and principles. We're turned upside down and then complain life is too difficult. If a dog were a cat, that wouldn't work well either.

Other things seem ridiculous too. There are television programs with very pretty and petite females who physically beat up large men. "Wonder Woman" is one thing, but in "real life drama," men act helpless, showing the world the "*power of a woman.*" This tells a woman they can get away with anything because a man would be committing a taboo by hitting a woman, and that men should take any abuse given to them.

I'm sure some females could whip a guy into the ground depending on the size and weight of each contender. Overall, it's a possibility, not a probability. My friends and I now hear some women use the jargon of "beating a man to a pulp" in casual conversation. It's another avenue of brainwashing the media provides to help make men become more passive and to avoid gender conflict. Are we getting the gist of it all?

## Protective Men

While in the military, I remember guys didn't want women on the battlefield or wherever combat was being fought. This included in the air, on land or at sea. It wasn't that men didn't want women in the military. Guys were adamant about keeping them from harm's way. Now, why do you think most men felt like this? I may have a hunch... because men are chauvinistic? I honestly don't think that comes close to the truth.

The reason isn't because a man thought a female couldn't shoot a gun or even kill someone. It's more serious than that. The reason is because *women were not created to be hunters, pursuers, protectors or providers.* They were created as nurturers, emotional support systems, caregivers and intuitive partners! Isn't it ironic hearing the same basic concept again? Let me explain this innate function using an excellent illustration.

Hunting and pursuing are two of men's innate qualities, be it the quest for a bride, or the tracking of animals or the enemy. When in battle, guys are one unit, thinking alike, going out to hunt, kill, protect their buddy, and get back to a safe haven. This complete male force moves forward. If someone gets injured, one or two men stay behind for a medic and then continue onward.

They keep pursuing the enemy and sense the like-mindedness and unity throughout the battalion or squadron. They feel everyone's emotion heighten simultaneously with their own. There is power, strength and direction because a comrade was injured. This unity provides purpose to each man, with the willingness to advance the enemy.

Now, let's assume the same scenario above with the troops moving forward to attack, kill and get back to their safe haven. We'll make a simple adjustment by adding one woman into the middle of these men. As you recall, the men were using only two of their innate virtues, hunting and pursuit. Now, they must add a third innate function of *protection*. They can't help how they're wired!

Prior to a woman amongst them, everything worked in unison with the proper virtues operating smoothly. Now, however, men have lost concentration on the objective of hunting and pursuit because the virtue of *protection* appears. They are concerned about her safety. Their priority shifts, so that she isn't hurt or killed above anyone else. Nonetheless, this goal may not be verbalized. Meanwhile, the enemy may become a bit wiser while protection of this woman is sought. On top of it, a woman may be weakened emotionally and/or physically by her monthly cycle. Men have never had this concern.

Some may think this scenario is dramatic and genuinely over exaggerated. Nonetheless, the point is plainly illustrated. This should say to us, "Yeah, a woman can go to war and fight, she can leave the home to work, she could try to balance her career, husband and children, or whatever else entices her. But, there are some costs in it all!" A woman should be able to do any of this, but it should be at the proper time and season of life. It should be *where* she can utilize her innate qualities to the highest degree.

Even though a woman may be able to do something a man does, it doesn't mean it's in her best interest, her family's best interest, or even her country's best interest. If innate powers of each gender battle each other without the thought of consequences, we end up in a situation just like today! If we think about it, many men aren't trying to be all powerful know-it alls. They have a place in the family and society, with some wisdom to know why things should be a certain way.

Good men are seeking godly women. In the meanwhile, the confused and undefined man is unable to love wholeheartedly because "his space" has been invaded. His innate purpose is being destroyed and eradicated, even though women say they want good, reliable and trustworthy men. His ability to provide lessens, as does family stability.

In the next chapter, we will define the power, position, and authority a woman possesses that no man could ever obtain. It's the total opposite of what a good man sees.

# Chapter 14

## The Power of a Woman

Have you ever realized the amount of power, influence, morality, and strength gathered into the depths of a woman? Have you noticed how the morals and standards of a woman influence men and how they perform? Have you seen the difference in children that have stay-at-home moms and the kids who don't? What about the stress a woman acquires from having to go to work and the health consequences she faces trying to juggle it all? Have you witnessed the loss of a woman's femininity as she seeks power and position in the workplace?

I'm not sure about you, but I cringe at the word "empowerment" used by feminists. It's like another goal has been attained to destroy another trait of masculinity in men, and that they're one step *past* gender "equality." I feel the word has hurt many innocent women and has blindly led them into the ranks of feminism without their permission.

Allow me to summarize this section first. *Someone needs to take responsibility and leadership to avoid sexual relations before the proper time!* It would be nice if a man took the reigns, but many are overwhelmed by their conquest and lack of self-control.

Knowing that many men are all about sex and reproduction, the issue of self-control needs to be addressed. Control is good when it's used properly, just as sexual relations are when they're entered into virtuously. Unfortunately, sex for a man and control for a woman are both used out of context. Let's try to straighten out the reigns.

Assume I ask Sue on a date and I try making sexual advances toward her. The first feminine action she could take is to say, "Sorry Jake. Find someone else willing to have sex because I'm not the one!" I understand her "no" means "yes," right? So, I either try to move in more convincingly or back off, *or* try to seduce her the next time we meet. If we do meet again, in more cases than not, I'll win my way.

Sue thinks refusing my invitation to a sexual encounter will scare me off. But, she also fears having no companionship. So, I get my sex. Why, then, is Sue angry with me? Actually, she's angry with herself in fear or regret of the decision she made. *Then her emotions are taken back out on me because her dream of sexual purity was shattered!*

The decision to sleep with someone, of whose past sexual history Sue has no knowledge, freaks her out! She doesn't know if it is a one-night stand, a one-month encounter, or a devastating trip for a broken heart a year or two down the road. *A woman's emotions were built for long-term… not short-term encounters!* This is why a *woman* must use her *gift of control* in the sexual arena *before marriage… Not in a marriage!*

Hence, *the "power of a woman" is directly proportional to the amount of personal self-control and adamant refusal of engaging in sexual acts, out of wedlock, with a man.* Scores of men hardly refuse an opportunity of non-committal sex from hardly any woman who offers! If a woman gives him sex, he has been given the ability to *control* a woman's emotions, immediate future, and long-term hopes.

Women know this across the globe. But, they're forgetting about the consequences of misusing this power that brings them frustration, grief, anxiety, hatred and confusion regarding their relationship with men. Sex was never intended for use outside of marriage. There has to come a time of realizing its sanctity, and just how powerful it is!

Men often use women sexually and break many hearts. Many women attain grief and have learned to return the favor. However, they neglect the fact they end up hurt, no matter what, if sex is involved. Men hurt also, but it is hidden more "efficiently" and deeper. They utilize their persona of "toughness." Then, from nowhere, a man's hurt is riled due to something a woman said or did out of her innocence. Without a doubt, his anger lashes back in one form or another. This will be clarified more in the next chapter.

After the fling Sue didn't want to have, another level of hurt has occurred. That is pregnancy. Now she's caught in the middle of a huge dilemma. For some reason, Sue opts for an abortion. Who's emotionally hurt for many decades to come? She is. Let's say she decides to keep the baby and dad runs off. Who is left holding the bag? Sue is. Is it clear that Sue *always* loses? What's ironic is that this heartache was totally preventable!

Do we see what's happening? A female may become troubled emotionally *after* the act of non-committal sex because she dreamt of saving it for a special man or moment. If her "dream" was shattered, she ends up nagging a man from now till doomsday! A man may become emotionally frustrated *before* non-committal sex, or lash back on the woman because he wasn't programmed on how to be intimate emotionally! He expects to go from "hello" to satisfaction with hardly any emotional investment.

In the end, a woman hurts mentally, emotionally, or physically, and reaps what she sowed in the beginning... *grief for not being respected sexually!* Fortunately, there are "action dads" who instruct their daughters on how to respect their body and control sex.

In contrast, other women or popular magazines may tell a girl to sleep with a guy by the third date, second month or whatever timeframe. These girls are pressured to stay up with the times because they are led to believe it is sexy, or that these timeframes are long enough to have learned a person's character! Otherwise, a girl will be an outcast if she tries to remain sexually pure. These girls aren't informed about the chance of pregnancy. They aren't informed about the possibility of dad running off, or maybe having to face the choice of keeping the baby or having an abortion.

I can't imagine, as a man, the awesome capability and responsibility of becoming pregnant and giving birth to a new baby. *It is power!* I've always seen a pregnant woman as beautiful, glowing, excited and happy. On the other hand, I can't imagine using my *"power of choice"* to go to an abortionist and allow him or her to terminate my baby. This "choice" is not supposed to be a method of birth control. We will look at the effects of this act upon both genders in Chapter 17.

Right now, however, many women must realize the rut they're in. It's a difficult one to get out of. Their wheels keep spinning deeper into the mud. They thought they were getting back at men decades ago, but they keep hurting themselves as they get older, and are found alone. They had chances with marriage once, twice, three or more times. What makes it such? Look at the patterns and I assure you that most of it is about giving themselves up to sex *outside the covenant of marriage.*

Men are just as responsible to control sex, but a woman usually can't rely on a man regarding this issue. One of man's foremost desires is sex, and he needs an understanding and loving woman to help him wait to partake!

Let's return to "my date" for a moment. If Sue told me I couldn't have sex on any of our dates, I'm now spinning *my* wheels in the mud. At first, I may try some sympathy to get Sue into bed. Maybe I'll try to seduce her with alcohol or drugs so she doesn't know what she's doing. If Sue stands her ground, I may get angry and leave, or I might just respect her for being up front with me and decide to treat her more appropriately.

If I persisted to seduce Sue, but she stood her ground, I would quite possibly leave to look for another woman who might please me. I make my moves and she says, "Get lost Jake." Suppose this happens again and again. Guess what? The power of women uniting and not allowing sex in a dating relationship will make me think twice about my motives.

Believe it or not, if a female uses her innate *power to control* sex before marriage, a male will have to find respect for her. He'll finally have to know her at deeper levels and vice versa! He's forced into a situation of respect, honor, and hopefully, real love. What's very important is that a woman has a male counterpart she can confide in; someone who supports her ambition and will help reinforce her desire. Dad would be the ultimate person, but if he is "unavailable," any male friend with the same deep conviction will do.

If a couple mutually talked about sex and what the experience might be like, the consequences that could occur and the financial responsibilities thereafter, they would definitely alleviate the pressure of having intercourse. The other person lets you know you're desirable. If respect is around, you will battle for the cause. If respect isn't around, you shouldn't be either! Usually, no one talks about sex respectfully; rather, it is often discussed in a distorted or perverse tone. Communicating candidly allows us to experience intimacy, mutual understanding, strength, and a feeling of self-control.

The first thing needing agreement upon in a relationship is that sex is postponed until we're positively sure marriage is on the horizon. After becoming friends, we should have a genuine *respect* for each other. If respect is attained, we won't want to indulge in something that will ultimately hurt or destroy the relationship. Following respect, we may realize our feelings have grown, and our sexual urges should drive us to the altar.

If we consider having sex before we should, be clear it's only a *mechanism that rejects rejection.* In other words, indulging in sexual acts before marriage, neither person wants to say "no" to the other, but if they do, there's a feeling of rejection. So, in order to avoid feeling rejected, sexual intimacy evolves. *We've rejected rejection by indulging in sex!* However, within hours we're dealing with guilt and shame. Now the good ole' internal conflicts are stirred, rousing confusion and a lack of peace.

Hormones are flying in the midst of seduction. Beneath it all, we just want to be close to someone who doesn't reject us like mom or dad did in years past. Maybe we had only one parent under our roof, and the feeling of rejection hovers over us. Maybe they never accepted us or told us they loved us, or they were very controlling. There may have been judgments, accusations, and prejudices that kept us at arm's length emotionally.

No one likes rejection. We were made to soar like eagles

and to have great health and prosperity. Many women have felt rejection and powerlessness for centuries, and they have wanted to soar. It is honorable to embrace freedom, and to experience life to its full potential. Unfortunately, many women have tail spun emotionally, physically and spiritually because of *over extending the boundaries* of their new found liberties.

The *Power of a Woman* I'm speaking of will adjust a man's attitude and actions. It will assist in creating a moral society! This power is connected to femininity, and femininity (along with masculinity) needs serious restoration.

If this *Power of a Woman* existed again, abortion would be virtually unnecessary. Divorce would significantly decrease because we would know the character of a person more thoroughly and avoid poor choices in a mate. Communication would be more intimate rather than couples arguing and running out. Men would fulfill their wives' needs more appropriately because opportunity to approach other women would fade. The single man would be forced to make a decision about his sexual appetite; he'd have to ask himself, "Do I want to pay someone for sexual pleasure or do I need to change my ways?"

Yes, women are powerful! Their innate power, via femininity, is unexplainable and real. They have the power to create new life and to train up a person in a way to benefit mankind. Women are God's daughters and feminine creations. He sheds tears over them because they've abused the power He's entrusted to them.

God favored women to be inspirational, intuitive, nurturing, and transforming. Women were given tools to help men understand relationship. A woman's power helps a man to seek out his true feelings based on love (*not lust*) by

131

enforcing laws of sexual control before marriage. It's painful to accept, but he's willing because he is truly in love!

Ladies, you were not created like a man; you were created with the same *human abilities* of a man. Your feminine abilities are the complimentary cornerstones lacking in every male. Your abilities are desperately needed in a culture that's been brainwashed by hurting women. Allow love of self to flow through you by first respecting your own body. Then, you'll reap the man who respects himself and who you are.

It's tough to change our habits in order to meet Prince Charming or Miss Right for life-long marriage. Our peers and the media throw much in our face. There's a remedy... find new friends and change the channel! Programming our mind with dishonorable T.V. shows expressing adultery or other evils allows it to transpire in our life. *"As iron sharpens iron, so one man sharpens another"* (Proverbs 27:17). Meaning: be selective with whom ya hang out with and what you watch, because it's what you'll become!

The point to grasp here, in the real world, is that a woman should intensely contemplate sexual activity beforehand because she is the one who may end up pregnant. She could end up abandoned by the father. She might have to face abortion, and her short term encounter may deliver long term emotional side effects. It would be great if single or divorced people practiced abstinence, not birth control methods, in order to maintain their *emotional health*!

## Searching for the Power

In the previous section we have addressed the reasons why a woman should want to control inappropriate sexual relations because of the consequences that may result. If it were all that easy by telling Jake to get lost, life would be pretty simple. However, if she is searching for the power of self-control on her own strength, it might be short lived.

Earlier we found what a man must accomplish in order to become godly. In order for a woman to use her power in an appropriate manner, she must also humble herself to God. How will she know if what a man says is godly, if she doesn't know herself? If a woman is single, who will she submit to? Is she just left out in limbo on her own because a man isn't in her life? How will a woman attain the power of control if God is forgotten? This reminds us why hierarchal priorities are valid, and having God in first position is imperative for both genders.

Becoming a godly woman will refine and define the feminine traits that she possesses. God will help rid her of the rejection, fear, anxiety, and stress that she has acquired. Our focus is not on worldly matters any longer, but spiritual ones. Making this transition is how love and peace are encountered. A "self-made," worldly woman doesn't always allow the power of God to create a lady out of her, nor will her power of control be as considerable.

The *power of a woman* will increase immensely when she realizes the *power of God's love within her.* In order for her to have the courage and strength to tell Jake to get lost, it requires a working personal relationship with Christ. When this occurs, a woman will expect a man to treat her appropriately, and like a lady, at all times.

Please remember, first and foremost, that both genders are accountable to God. It is *not* the total responsibility of a woman to control sex out of wedlock! If a godly man *respects, honors,* and *submits* to God's headship (*Chapter 8*), his woman will do the same for him! The combination of the *power of a woman with God's love,* and *a man's submission to God,* will bring the results that are pleasing to everyone!

# Chapter 15

## Jumping in the Sack too Fast

It requires faith, character, patience, long-suffering, and tenacity in order to obtain our heart's desire. Unfortunately, the emphasis of this wisdom is directed toward an individual's personal goals such as the military, college, and career or financial successes. When one or more of these goals are attained, we seek honor and respect. Nevertheless, this model seems to be neglected when it comes to lifelong relationship.

Jumping in the sack too fast as a single person doesn't mean marriage will never take place; it may take *years* before it takes place! A man's nature alone entices him to procrastinate about getting married. Add the fact he receives sex without total commitment, and he has every right not to marry. *It's sex that brings him back to his woman, not her dying desire to get married!*

If a woman finds a man with strength to sacrifice sexual relations for the benefit of life long relationship, she's struck gold! There are many guys who desire this, but are left behind. Today, some women pressure men to "jump in the sack" with the same non-commitment equal to many men. It's a "cake walk" for him these days. On the other hand, a man may regret sleeping with a woman in many cases. He wanted to respect her *and* himself, but the pressure of thinking she will leave him is too great to overcome.

Why do we believe that having sex before knowing a person's last name will gain us honor and respect? No matter what type of relationship, both men and women are ready to explore each other sexually. STD's don't bother them either!

135

It's on each other's mind to know if a disease exists, but they're too embarrassed to ask! Instead, hormones fly so fast, the sexual act becomes more obsessive than finding out if AIDS is lurking.

Deep wounds are created from premarital sex or infidelity. Initially, during the mechanics of it all, we're lost in the world of foreplay, other sexual activity, and the climax. The deepest concerns dealt with after a few hours of this sexual pleasure could be thoughts of pregnancy, the transmission of a venereal disease, feelings of shame, or that we may end up in a relationship we never intended to be in from the get go.

What a burden of worry to carry until a woman finds that her monthly cycle returned, that no symptoms of an STD surfaced, or that our freedom and finances are still intact. Our knees are worn out from praying each day hoping God has mercy on us one more time. Unfortunately, sometimes birth control and prayers don't work!

Nowadays, dating seems mechanical, from the personal introduction to having sex. There's often no emotion, love or commitment, and relationships are usually shattered because respect isn't demanded. If a person can't respect his or her body and health, how on earth will he or she find respect in marriage? "Jumping into the sack too fast" ensures a lack of respect.

It's imperative for a man and a woman to be friends first. If sex is experienced on the first, second, or third date, a couple goes from stage one to stage ten overnight. All the other stages of developing the relationship were denied. *They never got to know each other!* We can't skip getting to know a person! Sex is icing on the cake in marriage because we became intimate mentally, emotionally, and spiritually, *first*. Sexual intimacy allows celebration of our closeness in love. That is what sex was designed for and how it *should* be used.

On the other hand, having a friendship prior to any sex, would disclose any dark secrets someone else may have. When the time arrives, you're able to make *sane* decisions of whether you wish to pursue the relationship toward marriage or not.

Single women get emotional over losing their virginity soon after the act, or even years down the road. They realize it was their prize and gift for their future husband. A woman used to pride herself on that. *It helped capture a man!* Men wanted and respected a woman's virginity. In contrast, however, many men started to receive sex through their persuasion. After this happened, the promiscuous guy may have said he still wanted to marry a virgin. He really wanted to have his cake and be able to eat it too!

A person doesn't have the privilege to be sexual with anyone just because they're single or divorced. The complications created are never ending. In singleness, we're supposed to be a "servant" to others in need. It means we're to utilize our skills to assist our community, inspire children, and assist widows, or whatever else we're led to do.

God has always tried to warn us and spare us from the consequences of pre-marital sex and adultery. He told us that sex was intended for marriage, to flee fornication, and not to commit adultery. This wisdom isn't only to prevent unwanted pregnancy or to avoid venereal disease, but to *shun mental, emotional and spiritual chaos* if our relationship spoiled under natural causes.

Personalities, interests, priorities, goals, religious beliefs, culture, money, education, and so forth would fall under the "natural causes" category. The ironic thing is, if we didn't jump into the sack so fast, our friendships may still be intact! There'd be a stronger foundation for marriage, *or* our failed marriages might still be flourishing!

*"Flee from sexual immorality. All other sins a man commits are outside his body, but he who sins sexually sins against his own body. Do you not know that your body is a temple of the Holy Spirit, who is in you, whom you have received from God? You are not your own; you were bought at a price. Therefore honor God with your body"* (1 Cor 6:18-20).

## Sexual Transactions

Sex is pushed on us wherever we turn. The media knows it sells, retail outlets sell it, computers supply thousands of pornographic sites, the married and singles flaunt it daily, and our peers inform us of the swinger's scene. This only touches the surface. Unfortunately, with these pressures and temptations, many people fold. We face difficult situations and easily fall into a "sexual transaction." How do these transactions evolve?

I believe, within the first hours or days of conversation with someone new, it's difficult to keep small talk interesting. The choice to become vulnerable and disclose anything of substance begins to stare one or both parties in the face. To avoid talking about ourselves and getting to know the other person better, progression towards physical touch occurs if mutual attraction, chemistry, or hormones are present. Actually, these are *red flags* to prevent us from being wounded.

Instead of being human and exposing simple things that one person may want to share, the fear of past hurts, guilt, shame, and/or rejection begins to stir. Individuals lock up within themselves and cannot be intimate. Their disclosure could make the other person walk away if they said anything that might be "frightening."

In order to avoid rejection and shocking another person with his or her past, a man may lean towards sexual talk in order to escape disclosing his internal conflict. Many women also do this to men, but in all actuality the man is most guilty. He turns to his primary desire of sex, which he understands very well, and proceeds with seduction.

This playact is not condoned. Women need to understand and accept how men are wired so they can help control sex as mentioned earlier. Men need to understand and accept a woman's emotional wiring, in order to avoid creating a nagging wife or girlfriend, which may result from having any inappropriate sexual encounters.

Just because men are wired this way doesn't give reason why they should act this way. Remember gentlemen, women have needs also. They have emotional needs that must be met and rank as high as our sexual needs. So, which gender has the greater need? Exactly! Both genders have arrived at a level of *equality!* Thus, *needs must be met by the opposite sex, proving that we are equally deficient and not designed to do it all!*

Any man who seduces a woman (outside of marriage) in order to satisfy his sexual needs is selfish, disrespectful, and egotistical. Any woman, who uses emotional control to win her way, is just as deceitful.

Despite this, within the first few dates, sexual activity usually evolves, and redirects the relationship into a new dimension. By engaging in hasty sex, the focus is no longer on learning the character of the other partner, which is vital to long-term commitment. The couple's life now begins to form from the point of sexual closeness. It's like wanting to retire before graduating college. We want the prize before the sacrifice!

The process of learning the other person's feelings, acceptable habits, weaknesses, strengths, integrity and character is now muffled. Instead, everyday life with all of its problems and duties replaces the priceless learning curve. In any case, it's all about sex for the guy, and the woman is trying to hold him for the security she seeks.

Their concern becomes whether it was right or wrong to jump into the sack too fast. They've created a unique set of problems related to shame, guilt, or other ill emotions. The history of each individual's life becomes extinct in this relationship, relatively speaking. The woman becomes emotionally insecure from the sexual act and holds on *tighter* to the guy. The guy got what he wanted, and hides behind sex, knowing he will get it again and again. All the while, he holds on *looser* to the girl emotionally!

Subsequently, she questions why the attention, honor, and priority she seeks are extinct. After all, she's given him sex. What else does he need for her to become his number one priority? He wonders why she's become demanding and controlling, and why he isn't being *heard* or *respected*. It stems from the fact that they never united mentally, spiritually, or emotionally before sleeping together without a commitment!

Looking closer, friendship, intimacy, or romance wasn't established. They're aware of deep sorrow within and between them. The world isn't as bright anymore. Following a few days of celibacy, both people feel hopeful again, and believe they can redirect the relationship down the right path. Unfortunately, it doesn't unfold so easily.

Once uniting sexually, they got to *know* the other person at a deeper level. It's the unexplainable connection of knowing someone differently than before. It's like they see their insecurities and realize they had the strength to overcome the temptation in the first place. Now they are angry with themselves for giving into the temptation. Suddenly, there are mental, emotional and spiritual battles to live with.

The transference of each other's body and soul during sex is the profound *knowledge* I believe God spoke about when He referred to the *"tree of knowledge of good and evil."* Wow, that's a book of its own! We'll touch on that in a subsequent chapter.

Nevertheless, consequences shall be paid sooner or later for violating spiritual law. Besides all of the ill emotions, arguments, pregnancy and abortions that may occur, other results are experienced. The domino effect might lead a couple to repeat marriage with a divorce to follow, or they may split up and enter another relationship with identical unhealthy patterns! Each relationship creates more frustration and confusion.

Our inner voice tells us one thing and the world says something else. Remember, confusion is Satan's ploy and so are these transactions! And *"no,* the devil didn't make us do it;" we chose to do it. It was only an option contrary to God's!

My hopes in creating these thoughts, being right, wrong, or indifferent in your world, are to allow consideration of the sacredness of sex and the demanding responsibility and sacrifice to raise young adults. Being married limits us to one sexual partner. Being single allows us to "shop" for the person we desire to have as our lifelong sexual partner. We need to better understand our mate emotionally and spiritually before engaging sexually.

## How many people do you Know?

"How many people do you know?" I am not talking about business clients, friends, or relatives. I am speaking about sexual partners. You know how it goes. We start dating someone, get involved sexually, and go through some arguing and emotions. Then, after several months or years, there's a break up in a dating relationship or marriage.

The world says the best way to get over a person is to find someone new. So, we're on the prowl for someone else to accept our backlash from a previous relationship. This habit brings dissension to a new relationship because one partner may yell at the other for something their ex-spouse, girlfriend, or boyfriend was guilty of. The accuser doesn't realize they're blaming the wrong person. Their mind is engulfed with old software.

Out of innocence, Becky says or does something that Jim's "ex" had said or done in a past relationship that was hurtful to him. Jim's old programming kicks in and he lights a fuse because of it. Becky doesn't know where his anger or reactions came from. She didn't intentionally throw this at Jim. She was clueless. Nonetheless, Jim didn't realize his "ex" wasn't standing there when all hell broke loose, his "computer" reacted when prompted, and Becky received the download!

The world's way to get over someone is inappropriate. The suitable thing to do is eliminate serious relationships until we've *healed from, not forgotten,* the previous one! If a year hasn't passed, no one's ready. It seems hard to do, but if we aren't content and experience inner peace and solitude, we won't have long-term hope in any relationship.

Knowing too many people makes divorce fairly eminent. After a few years of marriage, a couple may get bored with the same partner. They acquire an insatiable hunger for somebody new and may end up experiencing an affair. They might have thought it was a one-time deal, but it initiates never-ending pain.

How many people do you know? How many people are subconsciously involved in your current relationship? How many "exes" are screaming in your mind? Why do you compare your last lovers with your new one? Why aren't you satisfied with anyone in your life? Why is your heart empty and your mind in constant turmoil? The reason is that we didn't heed God's advice and haven't taken the time to allow Him to heal our pain!

## Repercussion Alley

Satan's strategy is to lure people into his realm. We've just discussed a powerful route. Not only can the womb be impregnated, but the spirit and mind can be also, with every evil known to man. It originates from a current partner and their previous lovers.

When it's said that people sleep with more than one person at a time in monogamous settings, it refers to transference of spiritual matter from previous partners. Simply stated, you "*know*" the same people as your mate. Your new mate hasn't healed emotionally or spiritually from previous encounters. Thus, we experience grief because of it.

The result of our partner's promiscuity varies. Anger,

143

deceit, hurt, hate, revenge and other emotions arise. This is the spiritual effect. We may sooth our feelings with alcohol or drugs, but this may lead to other sexual encounters as the cycle gets more agitated.

As the cycle deepens with hurt, anger and bitterness, the craving for more intense sexual acts is played out. The cravings increase because immense lust overtakes the mind. It becomes more difficult to quench the thirst because of new twisted thoughts. These thoughts build upon the rocky foundation that's already been poured.

This routine doesn't only prevail in sexual areas. It's evident in alcoholism and drug abuse. It starts with a beer, but the hard stuff gives more satisfaction. Smoking a joint was cool until the effects weren't superior enough. Then Satan hands over more powerful drugs for a bigger high. We didn't want to do it initially because our innocence prevailed. That was the part to savor and protect! But, it's hard to resist while being pressured.

Some pressures come from parents who push their kids into these dilemmas. Either the parent literally supplies the paraphernalia to whoever is around, or the kids crave love and attention and find it on their own. Some parents will drink, or do drugs with their offspring. These are baffling circumstances. *Today's* children are our *future* and they need responsible parenting, as we had in years *past!*

We are all human beings and need spiritual rebirth in order to conquer the opposing forces. We *must* be reborn in spirit, through Christ, in order to fight the battle. Otherwise, we have no artillery to fend the foe. Hence, evil wins with a divorce, shattered career, or financial problems. Isn't this just the opposite of what our hearts desired in the beginning?

Why are we confused when God is nowhere to be found in our lives?

Parents have a duty to their child, society, and God, by taking responsibility for their choice to bear children. Parents need to stay married! Satan comes around and has taken mothers away from the home to allow extraordinary infiltration of ungodly spirits into the life of the innocent. The children, in turn, get caught up in whatever group, gang or activity that accepts or loves them. Nonetheless, Satan is clever and "rewards" everyone.

On the adult side, Satan rewards envy, greed, lust, covetousness, power, or whatever an adult might crave. This ploy derails parents from their most important responsibilities of raising their children. Money is the most important god in our culture now, and most people are trying anything to get it. So, they run for the gold and ignore the problem. People talk about the issues, but most don't seem to have the character to resolve them.

Believe it or not, the more people we "*know*," the more alcohol or drugs we "*know*," the more rejection we "*know*," or whatever else we "*know*," it weakens our ability to progress towards meaningful and lasting relationships. It weakens our stand against evil and our enemies. It allows injustice and immorality to prevail. Remember: *strong families, a strong community... strong communities, a strong nation. Broken families, a selfish community... selfish communities, a weak nation!*

Unwanted singleness and divorce results from too many ungodly sexual transactions taking place in both genders. They bombard our minds with lies and confusion, and destroy the relationship we desperately craved, and then the next and the next and the…

# Chapter 16

## Cohabitation: Defeating Commitment

In our modern day culture of sexual freedom, both genders enjoy the benefits of "equality" by engaging in non-committal relationships. If we think about it, prostitution and this lack of commitment are quite similar. I don't mean to sound insensitive, and I'm not trying to judge any man or woman. We need to contemplate the differences between these relationships, and compare them to current or past ones any of us have experienced.

It used to be true that only men wouldn't commit and females were quite disgusted with it. Now, both genders are disgusted! In a few of my own situations, there have been times I was accused of not committing, when in fact it was my mate's lack of commitment that ended the relationship. This frustrated me to no end. If I was non-committal, it was pretty evident!

Through this, I learned when someone accuses us of something we know we're not guilty of, *the person is expressing his or her own guilt.* So, instead of them admitting something wasn't right in their own life, our words of interrogation toward them are turned back on us until we hear enough false accusations. Then, we see them do exactly what we were accused of doing, or even worse.

I was usually made out to be the bad guy. Actually, I was a good guy, not bad enough! Girls always gave me the impression they could walk away void of any hurt. Well, if someone was never committed to a relationship, why would they be hurt?

In my life, commitment was never established for one reason or another. The result of my singleness is proof enough. However, it has never meant that I was unwilling to commit. If mutual commitment was established, neither I nor many others would be alone because the relationship would have experienced reconciliation. Unfortunately, choosing to cohabitate further complicates our lives, and commitment is radically defeated.

## Considering our Motives

We need to reconsider our motives before attempting marriage, having children, or cohabitating with or without a commitment. Cohabitation isn't the answer to ensure a marriage will work. It isn't a solution to paying the bills. Nor should it replace dating to see if two people are compatible so they won't have to divorce! This is insane.

In cohabitation, many forces work against a couple, and many end up in a worse financial, emotional, and/or spiritual condition. Sadly, a woman may feel she has won her man, and experiences a *false sense of security*, yet she is the most vulnerable emotionally. With all this, why do people think living together out of wedlock is socially acceptable?

I don't believe cohabitation is socially acceptable. It affects the minds of those watching it happen, and it devastates the minds of those participating even more so. They know deep in their spirit it's wrong. They're in constant struggle with their choice and what others may think. The prospect for peace and tranquility is banished. But, they block out the moral guidance they receive, and their heart becomes a little more "hardened."

Cohabitation arrangements are non-committal agreements that have pressures, consequences and societal penalties. These costs will certainly expose themselves due to the freedom of singleness that still exists while pretending to be married. Which is it? Is there commitment or not? If there's no commitment, then stay away from other people who may be committed. If both are committed, then *get married!*

Let's identify some social costs everyone waves their hat to: things like the public humiliation of good parents if their "properly raised" child lives with the opposite sex, or the personal grief parents have to live through because of what their kids are doing.

This doesn't promote peace and tranquility to these households. There is separation of family and friends. No one ever thinks of another person's feelings or dignity any more. It's all about "me" and the rebellion that is most suited for the occasion. It's often about spite and retaliation for something in which no one knows from where it stemmed.

Then, there is the financial stress. Government programs help these individuals when it doesn't work out or if there is an unwanted pregnancy. I know of children over the age of eighteen who have tried suing their parents for monetary support once they have left the house. These kids can't make it on their own with their unemployed girlfriend or boyfriend!

Thank God for parents refusing to rescue immoral situations! These poor people have heavy burdens placed upon them. Helping out these kids will hurt them in the short *and* long runs. Allowing them to experience some pain would be classified as "Tough Love." Maybe love has never been considered, but it's a disciplinary action for the good of the child's own self-worth, especially when they're twenty-nine!

## Perks or Consequences

The confusion of being single in a marriage setting produces much despair. Joe recognizes he is still "free" at a much deeper level than his "roommate" Jill. He actually feels the financial pressure dissipate a good bit because he's sharing expenses. It's only a "roommate" situation here with sexual "advantages" for him.

Jill feels more emotional security, and she expects relief financially. Sexually, Joe is most eager and Jill may fear pregnancy consequences. Nonetheless, she feels that "socially acceptable" options are available to her if the pill fails. The option of an abortion is actually more emotionally devastating and demoralizing than she realizes.

In the meanwhile, Joe feels anyone is still fair game to socialize with. If he's out with single male friends, they are "scoring" at the bars, beaches, house parties, and so forth. He's meeting up with new females, and finds no reason that he cannot pursue behind his "roommate's" back. After all, his "roommate" will understand because they are "only living together to reduce costs."

Jill, however, is taking a much more serious stand with their living arrangement because they are sleeping together. She expects the devotion and commitment that only comes in marriage when two people truly love each other. She never made sure he was more committed than her.

Once these perplexities surface in the living arrangement, more freedom develops in Joe. Now, he becomes less committed to keeping his promises, and starts getting home later than normal. He starts acting strangely, and arguments begin. All he sees is the mistake he's made and the trap he's in. He starts to wish he had never moved in with Jill.

All of a sudden, Joe has more opportunities of women at his disposal. This is due to the "security" he feels of having someone who cares for him... that *he* is *not* committed to! It's an ego boost to him because of the double mindedness that exists. He'll never lose at this point, he thinks. There's always Jill at home if the new girl he meets doesn't work out, at his "roommates" expense.

Of course, now he's created a nagging girlfriend. He can't take the accusations being thrown at him. He weasels out of the situation with soothing lies and tales that make her feel empathetic toward him. Now, the time comes to make up through sex.

Jill gets more attached emotionally because of sex, as Joe uses her in order to maintain his sex life. She feels having sex with him is the answer to sooth over any hurt that was created. Consequently, she doesn't realize that a relationship doesn't actually exist. Her emotions are all out of whack, and she can't see what's happening. This is where physical, emotional, and/or mental abuses permeate.

## Doomed Freedom
Joe really may not be having sex with another woman and says that he's faithful, but his heart is nowhere to be found in this relationship. Anger and resentment start building up in him because he hates being locked up in this living situation, since his freedom is now doomed. "Doomed freedom" in a man, when he is single, creates that anger. So, may I ask, "What has been achieved through this awesome living arrangement thus far?"

While having sex with his "roommate," his emotions

151

of anger are being taken out on her during the act. For a brief moment, after intercourse, his anger has been relieved. It had nothing to do with lovemaking. It's his anger being exposed through the sexual act that allows him to "beat up" his woman. Jill doesn't understand constant rough sex, while she seeks an emotional build up to make her even want to be with this guy.

"Doomed freedom" in a man isn't only evident in a cohabitation arrangement; it's also evident in a rocky dating relationship without cohabitating. Because the woman freely delivered sex, his needs are met, while she's still searching for some compensation along the way. Her needs rarely get met due to the lack of commitment on his part.

## Finance & pregnancy Issues

Finances start to become an issue as everything else is falling apart. The couple had it all figured out in the beginning. It would be so much cheaper to split the expenses. Well, all of a sudden Jill finds that Joe isn't working as much, or not at all. She's trying to support the household alone. She rightfully becomes angry over this fact.

Joe comes up with excuses of why he can't find a job. Yet, there's time to spend with his friends and party. Remember one thing: all of this has happened slowly, subtly, and deceptively over a period of time. Jill feels trapped. She takes the abuse and can't escape. Her need for security is threatened. She'd rather be in a bad situation than none at all.

The situation gets deeper. Jill ends up pregnant. Now what do they do? There is so much confusion, hurt, anxiety, stress, hatred, loneliness, and a score of other emotions that have developed over time. Jill realizes what a loser she's with. Now she has to make a *choice*, the choice to abort or not, because Joe isn't man enough to support himself let alone the child. She eliminates him from the decision of abortion as a means of birth control. She knows he won't be responsible financially, and she can't do it on her own.

Even though Joe might want the child, it will take much convincing on his part to change Jill's mind. He's already proven himself. Even though he wants the child and she goes through with the procedure, he cannot believe that she has ignored his requests to keep the baby. She tells him, *"It's my body and it's my choice."*

He is floored at such nonsense, and in all actuality is devastated. Even though Jill carries the baby, we must remember a man's need is to reproduce. He feels an attachment to the child as much as she may feel an attachment to the child in the spiritual realm.

There are ignorant, selfish, and intolerant men that are willing to afford an abortion for a woman. It's because of pride, fear, or to save embarrassment in front of his friends, family and peers. Women feel the same, it's natural. However, if this is "socially acceptable," why is it so difficult to make it public?

If Jill proceeds with termination, she's the one who lives with deep emotional hurt and pain. Joe moves on and experiences a brief instance of grief compared to her.

Lust, sexual impurity, lack of commitment, unmet expectations, anger, rejection, and bitterness are inhibitors of marriage here. The male has his sexual needs met which delays or forfeits any desire of marriage for him. The female becomes wounded emotionally due to unwarranted sexual activity, lies, or possibly from an abortion. If a break up occurs, her walls of resentment towards men will follow her wherever she goes.

Trust and respect have been hampered deeply if marriage does occur. Lifestyles haven't changed; old habits, emotions and friendships are still within a thought's reach. The same pattern of living still exists which fuels the fire for repeated arguments.

Getting married won't cure the fact that the guy doesn't want to work, or that the woman may not control her emotional upheavals. Maybe this is why cohabitation creates twice the chance of divorce than if we didn't live together before marriage!

### Television's influence on Morality

Television shows were rated "G" when I grew up. I witnessed extremely talented actors and actresses who left us with a moral message. We laughed because they were funny. Sex, language, or violence wasn't needed to entertain the audience.

TV Land still airs many of these programs. Can you imagine Herman Munster cheating on Lilly? Mary Tyler Moore telling Dick Van Dyke she's divorcing him because her girlfriend did the same to her husband? Or, "Little Joe" and "Hoss" cohabitating to see if things would work out before they got married?

This contrast is where we are today. Even though entertainers may have had personal issues off the set, the content being broadcasted went into the heart and soul of those watching. Society benefited from it, instead of it contributing to our detriment.

Slowly, subliminal messages were sent into our homes. "Three's Company" aired the first cohabitation arrangement. Sex, language or violence weren't involved. It planted a seed as we watched unmarried females and a male live together. Television's influence led the way to "acceptable" living arrangements today. Now, sexual acts are aired on major networks between the married and singles, or any combination thereof.

Archie Bunker didn't agree with the woman's movement. He kept trying to communicate simple truths about the creation of man and woman. Yet, his daughter Gloria and her husband Michael were trying to convince him that society was "behind the times," and that everything needed to be advanced equally among the genders. Now, we see how the roles of femininity and masculinity began to be subtly attacked.

I hope we realize the impact of modern television. It programs our minds with things that are destructive. Before eliminating cable TV, I used to watch TV Land every night for a laugh. I could relax and enjoy a decent show. Now, unless football is on, network television is too stressful to watch because it's hard for anyone to relax! At any second, the use of language, sex, or violence is used to "capture" the audience. Maybe, it is more appropriate to believe that repetitive "shock" is used to progressively desensitize us.

Advertisers really dumbfound me. They surround their commercials with sex, not the product. What they are doing is selling a porn site or girly magazine! They aren't profiting. That has been proven with the infamous "hamburger commercial" with Paris Hilton. Sales hardly budged! That sends a message, and maybe corporations will heed to *our* advertisement!

155

Morality has been "picked upon" for decades. In the midst of it, we are all paying the price by taking things into our own hands. Let's turn now to one "socially acceptable" procedure that fuels the fire of unwanted singleness and divorce. It is called abortion.

# Chapter 17

## Elements of Abortion

We hear devastating news reports about infidelity and abortion, referred to as an "ab." So, one day, I began research on women who experienced the process. I visited a website, *operationoutcry.org*, and read several affidavits of women who were asked questions about their experience. Two questions I focused on were the emotional after-effects on the women, and who pressured them into the procedure.

I created an emotional after-effects list. Some of the items listed were: depression, guilt, hatefulness, anger, aggressiveness, low self-esteem, denial, extreme anxiety, dependency on drugs or alcohol, grief, self-hatred, suicidal tendencies, being dishonest, lack of self-worth, and many others. Healing may never come if God isn't called upon.

I discovered that husbands or boyfriends were not as predominant as I thought in pressuring a woman to terminate a pregnancy. Parents, siblings, nurses, friends, teachers and social workers are all included. The array of people who counsel these frightened women was surprising. Sadly enough, most of the mothers felt they committed a crime after experiencing an abortion.

My naivety regarding those who pressured a woman was enlightened. Nevertheless, a woman is left to deal with the emotional effects for decades that no one informed her about. Maybe friends or family persuaded a girl to do something she never intended to do. Maybe the doctors and nurses lied and said, "There are no side affects. We aren't aware of any long term affects."

What about the men? They must have emotional side effects. Visiting another website, *afterbortion.com,* I discovered articles from men and women disclosing their experiences and traumas. Some men's emotions and behaviors ranged from a lack of self-esteem, to drug abuse, to feeling numb, depressed, argumentative, aggressive, and more. This site confirmed what women stated on the other site and went much deeper.

Husbands and boyfriends are sometimes "caught in the middle." In many instances they want the child. A man may grant an abortion because a woman will disregard his feelings, or she takes it into her own hands without his knowledge. Women proceed with reasons ranging from not wanting the child, to the interference with career ambitions.

It was rather time consuming to research abortion statistics. The information was endless and varied slightly from one source to the next depending on how the research was done, and the length of time it covered. Overall, the United States performs greater than 3,700 abortions per day. This includes both single and married women.

So, what's the conclusion? Recalling our list of emotional side affects on men and women, don't you think it's unlikely for people to "feel the love?" Every emotion stated is destructive and the wounds can last for decades. How can people search out a mate and not feel rejected? Tens of millions of people are spiritually disabled because of an abortion experience.

Most women who have abortions do so before the age of twenty-five. These poor girls are fragile emotionally and haven't even begun to live yet. Nonetheless, they can carry destructive emotions into a marriage, often leading to a divorce, or they may have no respect for men and end up being single. They often hide themselves in a career or whatever's safest. It's the same with men. They have other issues we've discussed, and have all this piled on top. The depth of this is frightening.

The deepest part of my soul believes this is how Satan does his dirtiest work. He prepares us by numbing our minds with drugs and alcohol, with disgusting movies and T.V. shows, pornography, lusts and sexual temptations. Then, we're so brain and spirit- dead, we step into situations repulsive to us. The finale is a jaded life through sexual pleasures most every human being desires, and is entitled to, under the right conditions.

Satan's scheme is so devastating that everyone and everything is affected. People who have experienced abortion have difficult times overcoming it, and if they do receive healing, most of their youth is gone.

Abortion is a colossal reason I feel *"Why Singles are not Married & the Married are Single."* Every devastating emotion experienced by a man or woman is encapsulated in one horrific act. Let's not focus on whether abortion is murder or not. First, we need to figure out why we're so miserable. "What came first, the chicken or the egg?"

### Profound Elements

Knowing what we do now, regarding the level of emotional side effects that abortion brings about in men and women, is it possible that we have lost our roles, femininity and masculinity because we can't see straight? These emotions are powerful with deeply rooted anger. When someone is angry, things can happen that they aren't aware of. This anger, however, is dressed over with careers, debt, unfriendliness, selfishness, poor work ethics, or striving for the impossible.

Have the forces propelling a woman's desire for "empowerment" been exposed? Maybe the word makes me quiver because it's only a mask worn by these poor women, in order to cover their pain of deep emotional issues with which they constantly struggle.

The truth is, "empowerment" is a deeply rooted internal conflict. Hence, the innocence, sweetness, fun-lovingness, altruism, and nurturing virtues and capabilities God intended for a woman to have, are being threatened or destroyed. Empowerment's secular purpose is exhibited through "sexual freedom" and "equality."

On the other hand, men have deepened their emotional struggle. We found earlier that they are not conversationalists, and they've been taught to be "tough" with "normal" developments in life. With this additional turmoil regarding abortion, it can only amplify a man's already fragile emotional state.

I believe we've discovered some profound elements. First, sex is a sacred gift to use within the confines of marriage. Second, we have seen the power of a woman misused, and the negative influence it has had on other women and society. We have discovered passivity and the lack of masculinity in men and how it has allowed anger to settle within them. Thus, the overall result reflects how the moral standards of men and women can destroy individuals or families.

Satan has worked triple overtime with extraordinary patience throughout history to destroy mankind. We are destroying ourselves by acting out the thoughts he places into our minds. Yet, God patiently stands by. He waits to award us with His love, and His ultimate plan of salvation, *eternal life* and *peace of mind.*

He's an *approachable* God. Don't let some religious notion make you believe He is an old judgmental man with a white beard and cane waiting to condemn us. This is another satanic lie, subtly planted into our minds, by religious authority and legalism.

Mom, please know that your baby waits for you in heaven. God is waiting for you to confess your wrongdoing. He wants you to ask for forgiveness and ask to be filled with His Holy Spirit, so that you may end up with your child for eternity. While still on this planet, He will give you new thoughts of truth, an awesome presence of His peace, and the power to defeat Satan and his kingdom of hurt, pain and lies.

The greatest "Heart Surgeon" in the entire universe wants to do a surgery on us. He wants to fix the heart and mind of every gender, race, creed and color. He even offers an insurance plan… He will never leave nor forsake us, and He gives us the promise of eternal life and a love and peace that shall surpass all understanding. Personally, I am not aware of any earthly doctor that provides any kind of insurance!

Perhaps it is time to take a moment with your Maker. He's anxious to heal your heart, and provide the love and forgiveness that you seek, upon your request.

# Chapter 18

## Men, Women and Pornography

Is it possible to discover the root source of pornography's stronghold on men? How did it evolve into the overwhelming problem that scores of men face and have to deal with today? Why is it difficult to be released from something so destructive? Whoever said it was a problem only men face?

Numerous men consistently make a deal with themselves and their Creator about breaking this demoralizing habit. Unfortunately, when a man makes an agreement to release from its grip at thirty years old, and still struggles with the fact it's no easier at forty, he can feel helpless and not know which way to turn. He's angry with himself for being stuck in a very private and personal matter.

Many single men admit that their life would be "perfect" if pornography didn't have to be dealt with. This temptation is usually a big deal and seems to triumph, no matter how they've tried to overcome it. Men fighting this dilemma remark, "If I only had a wife, I wouldn't live in this hell anymore." Even some women say the same... except wanting a husband!

Marriage, as we know it, doesn't exist in heaven. It's God's gift to us on earth. Nonetheless, some single men have carried this stronghold of pornography into their marriage. Since it wasn't dealt with properly and completely in their singleness, it has caused much havoc in their marriage, and their wife is clueless. Then one day, she isn't.

The Internet is full of pornography. It used to be that "porno stars" were caught in their own world of viewers. Now, innocent individuals might type in a website they thought was going to disclose information they requested, but instead, it's a porno site. The men and women baring it all are everyday people with a seared conscience.

Marriage was designed to keep men *and* women past the sins of the flesh regarding immorality. No other sin creates as much widespread damage, in such little time, with so much regret and hurt. There is no other sin that creates quite a large bank account in such little time either! *"But since there is so much immorality, each man should have his own wife, and each woman her own husband"* (1 Cor 7:2).

We know that within minutes of adulterated sexual delight, either partner may acquire an STD. A pregnancy may accidentally occur or even an abortion. Another man's wife may become pregnant from her lover. A divorce is filed because of it.

Sex is the largest and most powerfully misused gadget on the planet each and every day. Most men and women were created with an interest in sex and should enjoy it in marriage. Men and women welcome sexual intimacy for the most part, unless sexual abuse was experienced in one form or another. Like anything, sex can be used for *"good or evil."* In this case, pornography is evil and destroys many men and women. Emotional baggage continually increases.

In the case of a boy, sex is his weak spot because it's his strong desire. A girl's weak spot is security because it's her strong desire to feel protected and safe with a man. Thus, Satan involves the girl in pornography to rile the boy sexually and her reward is money. Everybody wins! If we gamble away morality, no one is left out of the jackpot.

We talk about men dealing with addictions to pornography. What about women who endorse it? Aren't they in these pictures? They may have been abused sexually in childhood, rejected by parents, or suffered other instances of abuse. They were brainwashed by the industry and convinced they would make gobs of money. Gender isn't the issue here. *Sex is our weak link.* So, marriage was to be our saving grace.

Any time we hear about relational issues at church, men seem to always be at fault, and then embarrassed in front of the congregation. Women are never brought into the subject; they are the victims, yet they are gravely involved. They escape without being addressed. Men are blamed for infidelity all the time. Infidelity isn't right. But, if a woman is found with a man, what is it called on her behalf?

Hence, if a leader discloses this delicate information, a woman may feel empowered a little bit more... the wrong way. She detects no blame on her part. She leaves the gathering feeling confident. Perhaps she reminds her man of what was said. This is so wrong. We are all human and we all need to clean up our acts. Blaming someone else for something we are totally involved in is hypocrisy.

A man may be upset because he can't overcome the grip of pornography. It's obvious that a woman hates for him to be caught up in its vileness. We know the viewing of this stuff in the wrong man's eye can lead to violent crimes. Even so, scores of men may approve of their sons to view this sexual material.

Some men will say that sexual relations "make you

165

a man" before becoming a teenager, or shortly thereafter. Some moms have no regret of their daughters baring their body. Many females dress provocatively with nothing left for a man's imagination. There is such widespread indecency; it has now created desensitization in our culture.

A woman's attire, or lack of it, can drive a man to a pornography site. The "tease" he sees on the street plays in his mind, knowing he won't get what's waved in his face. It's another form of rejection. In time, his anger showers on a female. Normally, it isn't strangers who get hurt… it's his family or friends. So, yes, it does matter how every man's daughter dresses!

I loathe the fact that men have this despicable problem to face. It affects every part of their lives, and especially their families. I detest the fact that many women fuel the fire, and then complain about a man's ways. It seems these women won't recognize their part in it, and will continue to participate without remorse.

Self-respect is at a loss and is spreading like wild fire. Society has made morality so immune that the ungodly power of a woman is being used to destroy not only marriage relationships, but also other innocent women. We need to witness a dividing line again between the godly and ungodly! There is a moral dilemma out there without question.

Pornographic material usually arrives in a boy's hand at a rather young age. Girls are influenced at young ages also. It's in their *moral innocence* where all of Satan's work begins to twist their minds. Remember, Adam and Eve had the "Life of Riley." They were in their *moral innocence* when Satan began to twist their minds!

## Sexual Imprints

As a boy grows and views a pornographic magazine, film or website, his innocence is being destroyed. He *"knows"* something is enticing and desirable even at a very young age. Once viewing a naked woman in any of these forms, or in real life, his mind has been "sexually imprinted." A picture has been snapped and remains on the negative of his mind. He has an image of how a woman should look to him from that moment forward.

Once the imprint is established, outside of marriage, it can destroy his relationships, self-esteem and respect for a woman. This is why virginity is sacred. A husband and wife's initial imprint of each other is stamped on their minds. It is all they *know*.

If the first imprint in a boy's mind is a small-breasted woman, he carries this picture wherever he goes. He's fascinated at his first view of a naked woman either in the flesh, or in print. It becomes part of his search and desire in a mate. As he begins dating, his first girlfriend happens to be well endowed. Without reason, the relationship fails.

One reason it may have failed is due to the fact that the initial snapshot of his first girlfriend's figure doesn't match his deeply imprinted mind. His comfort level and expectation hasn't been met. He just isn't happy with what he has. Waiting for marriage in purity, each spouse's imprint is all they should ever *know*.

Regarding marriage, the power of imprint between two virgins will remain etched in each other's mind. If a man's wife was slender on their honeymoon, and then she gained weight, her husband's snapshot battles in his mind. Thus, sex may become a lesser pleasure in the marriage and may lead to an affair with the *initial imprint*, not necessarily an attractive woman! This may be why a wife is confused and says, "You've got to be kidding, I'm prettier than her!"

Another impact of a first imprint is when a person feels unable to achieve what is being portrayed in a pornographic photograph. Something may be viewed making a man feel inadequate to please a woman, or vice versa. This type of imprint can lead to a life long battle of disappointment, frustration, or feeling unable to please someone sexually.

If either or both of the individuals have been with other sexual partners before marriage, there are more problems to deal with. We spoke about this in "How Many People Do You Know?" This is another basis for why I believe adultery is at an all time high, accompanied with divorce. It could be that one or both of the spouses have sexual imprints they favor over the one they married. It might result in an "open marriage."

Women have acquired sexual imprints also. This is why it's easier for me to believe that many sexually abused women don't know the difference between love making or selling their bodies for sex. They're only familiar with their first experience, or imprint, with a demented male. Hopefully, this allows another practical view for us to consider.

These experiences often lead women into abusive relationships. Their judgment is obscured in the selection of a spouse. It is no fault of their own; it's what they *know.* Thus, they'll attract a similar type of man who displayed no respect to them because of familiarity. A woman may not be content subconsciously if she isn't yelled at or abused somehow. By the time a woman realizes she doesn't have to put up with it any more, mental, emotional, and/or physical abuse has already occurred. Physical beauty, or lack of it, has no value on the slide rule.

Consequently, pornography may be a huge sponsor to this abuse. Pornography is a rotten, shameful and indecent attack on many cultures, and it infiltrates deeper every day. It's an accepted piece of terrorism destroying mankind. Nothing is more "*good or evil*" than sex, depending on how it is used.

## Realizing spiritual Truth

We must realize that there is an intense spiritual battle going on. Satan blinds men and women in order to build his army while God builds His. However, Satan's side is more attractive and fun for immediate pleasure. He knows how to attract and destroy, which is his purpose. God's purpose is to attack back, through prayer, worship and warfare. It's accomplished with the indwelt power of the Holy Spirit we've asked for. But, this requires faith and tenacity.

Satan knows the power of sex. He involves women at a level to distract men because man's innate desire is sex. Many women get into this business for money to support a child, get through school, or because they have no education. Many have been bribed in their innocence, and the imprint they have received has been damaging ever since.

Now you ask, "How did these women get bribed in their innocence and where did they get their imprint?" The straightforward answer is *man.* The specific men I am referring to are their dads or male guardians. These guys never experienced self-respect, self-control, acceptance, love or manhood. They were pushed through the system of growing up by their dads, who never knew how to have relationship.

Many men are upset with their dads for not advocating their accomplishments and failures, or they experienced no communication of their dad's love. Maybe dad didn't support his son's sports or other activities. Maybe discouragement or demeaning statements were received from dad.

Even though dad may be present, he can still be absent. *Most every child* without a father becomes a victim in life. His offspring carry their internal conflicts into personal or working relationships. The child can't stay the duration because of a lack of self-worth.

Unfortunately, down life's road, anger is often lashed out toward females. They are weaker physically so these men get away with abuse. Satan's influence absorbs these men's minds. The darkness that overshadows a man allows disrespect through rape, incest, or other kinds of abuse. It's a sick way for a man to be heard regarding his lack of love.

The "macho/tough" guy feels desperately unloved. He acts tough without any emotion because his father never displayed any to him. There was never any soothing affection or love given to him by his dad. Without warning, he starts tearing apart on his insides. He can't understand why he feels so hardened. It feels as if his whole mind and body is an armored tank. Then, when a man marries, he still can't "feel the love."

We have a conclusion! *Men are the reason men are tainted! Men are the reason women are tainted! Men are tainted because they haven't been pulled aside to learn relationship!* The ones teaching this should be women. But, women can't be teaching men how to have a relationship with any respect toward them by removing their clothes at the drop of a hat! Somewhere, individual responsibility needs to help solve this.

Pornography doesn't help men solve their sexual craving. It is only a catalyst to a greater suppression of sexual energy, without physical touch, that builds a much angrier man. He may achieve a release from the flesh, but his mind and emotions still seek peace and satisfaction. His desire is the soft touch of a woman. A magazine, film, or website can't provide this. A female "star" has no idea of the torment she puts a man through.

This is why I believe pornography may lead to violent crimes. True relationship happens if a woman demands respect from a man by not allowing sexual pleasure before the time is due! Women should demand hugs, affection and respect toward their body by reserving it for marital pleasure. Men should stop thinking they're *entitled* to sex because their libido is roaring like a tiger.

Another subtle impact many men forget about is an airbrushing technique used in magazines. It allows a woman to display perfect skin, hair and makeup. Some models are literally pieced together with someone else's legs, face or other body parts. They aren't real! Nonetheless, everyday women spend thousands of dollars to try and look perfect.

Now some men expect perfection. They demand a facelift, body lift, breast implants, or whatever else they find attractive from these pictures. As time passes, the erotica a man views doesn't quench his thirst. His sexual appetite increases with deeper levels of pornography being sought. *Spirits of torment* are riling a man through a woman's demise.

171

## Helpful hints for men and Women

Men struggling with this issue can't continue to hide and believe it isn't affecting their marriages, jobs, girlfriends, congregations, the lives of their children, or even their own destinies. Maybe an addiction has developed that's being denied. Having instant access to these pornographic websites magnifies the problem. As with any addiction, admittance is the biggest step of all. Once we are honest with ourselves, steps can be taken to heal.

Once a problem is admitted, a person might recall loathing the habit in the past. At the time, they thought victory was near, but temptation overcame them by replaying the "enjoyment" they received from it. When this happens, a sincere desire to retreat needs to resurface by dumping the computer, get an ISP that blocks pornographic sites, or have someone put parental locks on sites frequented.

The most difficult step is to disclose our secret to someone we trust. Hopefully, this will be our significant other. If not, we should start where we're most comfortable. There's nothing wrong with confession to open the door of healing. *"Therefore confess your sins to each other and pray for each other so that you may be healed"* (James 5: 16r).

Even though we confess, and no one wishes to honor our confession, we've done our duty. Satan detests our confession. We could experience judgments from the person we disclosed our secret to because we spread light into the dark. The war has begun! God will judge accordingly.

This is why a personal relationship with God is rewarding. He always forgives us no matter what! We receive unconditional love! Nonetheless, He doesn't allow blasphemy of the Holy Spirit. *"And so I tell you, every sin and blasphemy will be forgiven men, but the blasphemy against the Spirit will not be forgiven"* (Mat 12:31).

Nonetheless, if a man approaches his wife or girlfriend to confess, it isn't her place to judge. Maybe she should disclose her dark secret in unison! If he approaches, he truly wants to conquer this horrible curse. He's saying he's sorry, he loves her, and wants help. If friends or significant others are not the answer, spiritual counselors are waiting.

Remember, gentlemen, we're hurting the women who love us by not taking control of what other women throw in our faces. We don't have to look upon every female with lust. We can look at a woman with respect, and appreciate her beauty when she displays herself properly. Then, we should go home and be with the women we married.

At the same time ladies, realize the pressure you're putting on men. Deposit some clothing on your bodies, inspire younger girls to be godly, find the power to control sex outside of marriage, not in it, and remember, a little bit of class reaps respect from men.

Most people have "open minds" about sex. Maybe it's time to close them and put sex back into the confines of marriage. Our families and communities would be the beneficiaries!

# Chapter 19

## Quest for Beauty Queens

Many men hope for a "Beauty Queen" as their future wife. It isn't uncommon for a man to seek this type of woman. It is his innate desire. With most attractive women, however, it seems that some sort of attitude and/or entitlement combo that we have already discussed in Chapter 12 muffles their radiance.

Male counterparts have discovered the most *approachable* women are typically from other countries. It's pleasantry to receive a smile, a hello and to witness femininity. It's nice when a man doesn't have to feel defensive or "outsmarted" at first glance.

All types of men regardless of the man's education, salary or emotional health approach these types of women. Men gravitate towards them because the woman's demeanor is calming and down to earth. Because of it, seduction isn't in the forefront of his mind, and the girl gains respect. This has nothing to do with the size of a woman!

I, like many other men, am usually drawn to a pretty woman. It's natural and without an agenda. Many times, however, men are too shy to approach them, and these women may end up compromising their own dreams of a man because of it. Nowadays, it is difficult for me to approach someone because I don't know if I can afford her financially *or* emotionally. *In the back of most men's mind is the issue of "affording love" rather than affording a family.*

Nonetheless, men have been doing something about

lost values. They've gone overseas to find a wife with old-fashioned standards. It used to be that only military men met their brides abroad. Now, I'm surprised at the number of men participating stateside.

By doing this, men find their beauty queens. These women possess femininity, are supportive of their man, and they voice words of love and commitment. Although they work hard, they don't prioritize career, and they believe in a strong family and traditions.

Some of these marriages don't work for one reason or another. A few women want a free ride to the U.S., or some men feel like they can treat them as slaves because they are subservient, and forgot they are humans with dignity. Nonetheless, a man takes a fifty-fifty chance, as she does. But, these odds are *better* than marrying someone from home!

In general, European women are well educated. The difference is their hierarchal priorities. They talk about loneliness and needing protection. They talk about morals, values, and doing whatever it takes to make a marriage successful. They talk about romance, strong men, and children. But, with many having faced war, or the lack of freedom on their streets, they know about priorities.

The U.S. used to be a leader in many moral arenas. But, as teenage pregnancy in the U.S. has doubled or quadrupled compared to other developed nations, I think we have lost some ground. Morals need to be pumped into parents, and parents need to energize their offspring with some of these values.

There are several opportunities to seek a relationship

every day. But, it's difficult taking a girl seriously, as wife material, when she walks around dressed with everything hanging out. There's no class, dignity, self-worth, or pride displayed. It might be time to straighten up hierarchal priorities. That would repopulate our "Beauty Queen" arena!

### Surgical Repercussions

In a single episode, "reality" television broadcasts the reconstruction of a woman's body from head to toe as she tries to become a beauty queen. The costs are not felt physically, financially, or emotionally in our living rooms. It is the "micro-waved" era of Satan putting lifelong burdens on parents and children in order to destroy contentment.

For example, a teenage girl stated in a local newspaper that getting breast implants was no different than whitening her teeth! Lord help us. By the time many adolescents reach seventeen or eighteen years of age, they have already experienced marital pleasure, have their own sports car, and have traveled to every corner of the earth. What will these girls and boys have to look forward to in their twenties and thirties? Marriage?

Have you read any articles stating possible repercussions from breast augmentation at young ages? Some of them are hardness of the nipples, wrinkling of the skin around the implant, loss of sensation, interference with producing milk for mom's newborn, brain cancer, and usually some maintenance within the first five to ten years. Why is this difficult to understand? What are the long-term effects?

A girl's "happiness" is temporary. The physical pain she experiences for several weeks is one payment for her short-lived "happiness." Girls say it's not done to attract the

177

opposite sex, and I'm now beginning to believe it. Being "hip" is dangerous today.

I thought a woman's monthly cycle or pregnancy enlarged her breasts naturally. I thought physical imbalances were corrected, or even over corrected by nature, in pregnancy. These "imbalances" and clothes not fitting prim and proper are reasons why many girls want implants, according to a news article.

Have you ever looked at your face? It's imbalanced! One eye may be smaller than the other, or your smile may be crooked. Many people walk with one shoulder higher than the other. This is natural stuff. We are not perfectly balanced!

It's rather ironic that I don't know of any man who likes implants! I'll say this: men like to see nice figures and their eyes will usually catch them. However, given the choice, most men prefer a soft and natural woman. Augmentation changes the mind of a girl. It's the attitude/entitlement syndrome working. Thus, a single man may innately avoid a "plastic" woman because she carries herself in *fleshly pride* rather than in *godly security*.

Plastic doesn't allow human connection. There's interference in the transference of touch. It's like a wall you cannot get through. Emotions are affected, and become surfaced. A man may look upon a woman differently with a slight loss of respect. Guessing games engulf his mind wondering if she is "real" or not. For me, I've finally come to realize, "if it's too good to be true, it is!"

Small, medium or large breasted women are all sexy! It was Solomon's wisdom that encouraged a man to be happy with his wife's breasts! *"A loving doe, a graceful deer – may her breasts satisfy you always, may you ever be captivated by her love"* (Proverbs 5:19).

Then we read… *"Do not cut your bodies for the dead or put tattoo marks on yourselves. I am the Lord"* (Lev 19:28). Man, did God have us all figured out or what? I suppose if He said not to do this, it must be connected to paganism.

There was a news report on T.V. about a woman who got a face-lift. Her husband wasn't very supportive of the idea. Nonetheless, she had the surgery without considering his feelings. Afterwards, her husband felt he lost the woman he married because he felt *her whole mindset changed* after six years of marriage. Prior to the operation, he was content with his wife's appearance. Unfortunately, after the surgery, and some major disagreements, the couple divorced.

Some may think this is a lame excuse to divorce. I would agree if it were all focused around the surgery. However, I would have to believe there was instability in the marriage prior to all of this. She may not have felt loved, and he may not have felt respected. Unfortunately, this couple discovered serious consequences by ignoring some internal conflicts they never dealt with before getting married.

Plastic surgery, abortion, divorce, bankruptcy, or other life changing trends are necessary at times. Nonetheless, if we use these options due to low self-esteem, rejection, feelings of inadequacy, or judgments, we may end up in a worse situation.

Women with breast cancer should be candidates for implants. A woman assaulted sexually, or a mom whose life is at stake delivering her baby should be able to opt for an abortion. If a married couple has exhausted the processes of reconciliation, divorce is an option as a last resort. If after several years our finances are upside down because of a devastating life change, accident or medical condition, bankruptcy may be the answer.

These are godly options *under the right conditions!* Unfortunately, implants are often a source of self-esteem and happiness, abortion is usually a birth control device, divorce has an array of unfit reasons to occur, and bankruptcy is often a tool for those making tons of money that can't control their spending habits. Categorized, this would be referred to as *spiritual* bankruptcy.

### From dreams to Fantasies

As a teenager, I dreamt of meeting Miss Right. She was beautiful, had a big heart, and was caring. She was down to earth, feminine, and had a good deal of common sense. I envisioned a virgin and our wedding night was going to be special. I was excited for this woman to be in my life. My dream wasn't far fetched because these were the types of women I was surrounded by growing up. It was how I was programmed.

Nonetheless, when coming up through the dating ranks, I remember my dream fading. At first I admitted, "It's OK if she isn't a virgin... most aren't anymore." Dating a little more, "Well, it's OK if she isn't a virgin just so long as there's no STD." A little further, "It's OK if she isn't a virgin, doesn't have a venereal disease, and if she's divorced only once, that's OK too." A couple of more experiences, "It is OK if she isn't a virgin, doesn't have a venereal disease, and it is fine if she's divorced with kids."

I am not trying to ridicule these women. I'm saying

that I saw myself compromise my expectations one girl after another. Since I was unable to attain my "dream girl" in my youth, *my dream had carried forward and was converted into a fantasy!* I struggled to find "Miss Right" because my programming was not compatible with the new software that was trying to be downloaded. I kept fantasizing about my once *valid* dream because my imprints constantly reminded me of what truly used to exist. This has contributed gravely to my being single. It is why many of us are *"Caught in the Middle"* emotionally.

There's another group of lonely people who never expected their dreams to be shattered. They are the single moms and dads. Any time I attended a single's event, I anticipated never married singles to be abundant. Unfortunately, this wasn't the case. The odds turned against those seeking similar marital backgrounds in the never married realm.

Our homogenized society has provided greater opportunity for bedroom pursuit because of it. Younger men are usually concerned with how much sex can be had without commitment. So, divorced women become their prey because they're "easier" to seduce than single women. Usually, everyone's needs are met for a few weeks of satisfaction.

On the other hand, a girl in her teens or twenties is hoping for Prince Charming to arrive. However, he's having too much "fun." Nevertheless, he believes the young beauty queen will still be there when he's done, and his dream will still come to pass.

Once a man reaches his thirties, there's a struggle with being single because most of his fun is over. The sweet thing in her twenties is nowhere to be found. Deep inside he still believes his dream girl (who's now a fantasy) will still show up. She doesn't appear, but there's still enough youth left in him to attract a woman for a "roll in the hay."

As he grows older, he's dealing with career choices. He can't afford a relationship because his libido took priority with emotional side effects and destroyed him spiritually. He gets stuck in the corner without a woman, yet he still wants the "real thing." Now, later in life, he has to straighten up financially to become desired by the opposite sex.

There are consequences to having "fun" outside of marriage. We may end up alone, while all of our dreams have converted into fantasies.

# Chapter 20

## Finding the "Real Thing"

Infatuation focuses on the positive attributes of a person that will eventually wear off. These attributes could be a person's looks, money, power, car, status, etc. Remember, impressing someone else in order to "catch" them is what we are dealing with here. It has nothing to do with love, "the real thing."

We've always heard that getting married will make things worse if our dating relationship was bad. We hear how difficult marriage might be when things are good between the couple. Why is that? Why is it that after a marriage is consummated, things might go south in a hurry? Even though couples discover these statements are true, it's still hard to grasp what happened.

Let's say for example, a specific woman meets this guy and admires his physique and the car he drives. He thinks she's the prettiest creature on earth. So, he asks her out and they begin dating. The "feelings of love" come to surface and hormones start flying. During the first several months she enjoys his company and activities. He takes her out to dinner, movies, and plays golf with her. He also participates in the things she enjoys.

They realize how well things are going and their "feelings of love" are just as strong nine or ten months down the road. They decide to marry within the next two months. So, at twelve months they tie the knot, and life is good early on in the marriage. Before you know it, things start looking much differently on the other side of the marriage contract.

Nonetheless, the husband wonders why his wife isn't participating in golf anymore. She's confused why he won't get off the couch unless he plays golf! He was not a couch potato, and she enjoyed golf before they married. Suddenly, two different people appear under the same roof.

What happened to the romance and activities they enjoyed doing together? Simply put, they were both putting their best foot forward during the stage of infatuation. During this stage he's trying to capture the girl, and the girl is trying to win his heart. The whole stage of infatuation can last on an average of eighteen months.

Until this stage has been traveled thoroughly, people don't know if they truly *like* the other person. Only when infatuation has faded, and real life takes a toll will a person know if their relationship is one for marriage, friendship, or two people passing by. Many people marry the wrong person because their decision is based on the "feeling of love."

Traveling the road of infatuation, we'll be able to determine if the other person loves us more than we love them, or if they are more committed than we are. It requires real life experiences between a man and woman to test the character of the other. This means it takes time! Every relationship has to go through the proper stages in order to build a strong foundation. Eighteen months sounds like a lot of time to make sure you're with the right person. That slips by fast if you enjoy your friend. But, compared to a lifetime, it's nothing!

Many single adults in their thirties and forties have never married. Finally, when they feel they've met the right one, they're engaged within months. Two people might hit it off fast and know in their hearts they found the one, but what about enjoying some time together, or meeting their friends and family? There are habits, favorite foods, and hobbies to discover. This won't happen in a month's time, no matter how you feel. The urgent need to be engaged doesn't have a very optimistic future, especially if desperation is involved.

We all need support to have a lasting marriage. We all need great advice from successful people in any arena of life... especially marriage. Once we find someone with sustained character, respect, trust and mutual attraction, then we can head to the altar for the "real thing."

## We should change, not Them!

Two of my physical desires in a woman are that she's attractive to me and she takes care of her health. Two spiritual qualities I seek are femininity, and the godliness she possesses through her actions, not by her words. If I can't find this in a woman, should I try to change her?

I've always believed in seeking qualities in someone that I can offer myself. If I was a hundred pounds overweight and wanted the same slender woman, then something's wrong because I'm unable to offer it back. I'd be out of my league. Why would a healthy woman want to be around me? Nonetheless, I may go through life expecting something that's never going to happen. A lot of men expect a super model when they've never lifted a weight or ran around the block! We're dealing with those fantasies again!

Overall, I've taken care of myself and have been blessed with awesome health. It's hard work to maintain. So, let's say I meet someone out of desperation, loneliness, insecurity or other ill emotion. I'm attracted to her, but she's overweight. Her feminine qualities are intact, but she talks about God instead of putting His wisdom into action.

185

I say, "That's OK. I'll help her lose weight! I know she loves God, I'll teach her to be more action oriented. Then she'll be exactly what I am looking for!" Hence, the struggle begins to help her lose some pounds and act godlier. She's doing really well and I am proud of her. A few months down the road, I notice her figure disappear as she starts talking the talk again. Before you know it, she's right back to where she started.

The point is, *we should pressure ourselves to change, not them!* If we're pumped up to change them, it's only going to be temporary. If they change for us, their efforts may be linked to the infatuation stage. People try to live up to another's standard in order to hold on to them. Unfortunately, if it isn't part of their make-up, it will never work out.

Many times I recall girlfriends saying, "Your standards are too high. I'll never be good enough." After thinking about it for years, I came to realize that I put a lot of work into myself. I am not walking around thinking how "great thou art." I'm just being me.

Nonetheless, I received biased judgments and false accusations from some women saying I had "no heart," and that I was trying to sleep with any female I met. Finally, I saw the women who were saying these things. They were the ones who didn't take care of themselves in one way or another. To me, taking care of myself is natural or normal. To them it was a threat. My best relationships were with women who did take care of themselves, and I wasn't condemned for who I was.

People always make improvements to themselves. They'll enjoy long lasting effects if it's done on their own accord. It's different seeing someone achieve something because of a strong inner conviction. It is done out of self-love and self-respect rather than trying to live up to some standard that isn't within their reach.

If someone completely changes for our happiness, they've left their happiness. If they aren't happy, they're probably bitter or resentful, and our happiness was only temporary! I can't believe this is a healthy way to live and prosper in love. Do you?

Sometimes real love motivates a person to improve in areas they feel deficient in. We hear about extreme weight loss, spiritual revival, careers getting back on track, natural makeovers and a slew of other things. Love is a healthy motivator to accomplish these goals if it's truly "the real thing."

Otherwise, we need to make sure we know the long-term emotional, spiritual, mental, and physical patterns of a person before saying, "I DO!" Cohabitation is not the answer to discover these things. Allowing someone space, and learning their character, will foretell their devotion in every area we are interested in.

We have to be honest with ourselves in choosing the right person so we can be our true selves. It may take longer for a mate to come along, but we need to stop bouncing from one relationship to another because of loneliness and insecurities.

## How will I Know?

The most frequently asked question in finding a life-long mate is, "How will I know?" We want to be sure the person we end up with is "the one." Nevertheless, all sorts of *insignificant* signs occur telling us that they are the "one."

For example, if today we pray for our spouse and tomorrow we run into somebody, more chances than not, they aren't the one. If we meet someone whose name we adore and they make us tingle, they're probably not the one. If we got online and meet twenty people and had to choose someone, I am sure they're not the one.

Most people, meeting under these conditions, love the idea of love. They envision their whole life with this person after the first date, and don't have the slightest idea of who they are. If they get involved and it doesn't work out, they blame God, get to hate the name they once adored, or find out that the computer generated person had way too many problems to deal with. People fall in love with the *idea or emotion*, not the person.

The only way to know if they're the "one" is after infatuation. *Both people must know intuitively that the other person is as committed as themselves in their relationship before getting hitched!* Let's analyze this statement further.

The understanding to grasp is this. Infatuation needs to dissolve first; we need to know we aren't falling in love with the idea of love. Since we know ourselves much better than the other person, we realize deep within that we would never give up in a relationship, no matter what. We are a whole person knowing there will be tough times, arguments, adjustments, some selfishness, and other human conditions.

Within ourselves, we're ready to please the other person by being sacrificial to their needs or requests by using our wisdom, and sticking to healthy boundaries. We trust ourselves deeply, and know that we'll rise to most any occasion. However, the question is, can we trust the other person with the same deep commitment that we feel capable of and willing to provide?

It's difficult to know the level of commitment the other person is at or willing to go. We don't know if they have a personal agenda or not. Therefore, we have to learn the person! The *only* way to learn them is by observing their levels of respect, communication, character, and integrity. We need to learn how much they care about us before allowing them in a little deeper, and before saying "Yes" to marriage.

In other words, we mutually check each other out over a period of time. We want to know they have the stamina we carry in many situations or conditions. We know we'll go the distance, but will the other person make up the distance and maybe pass us by every now and then? Thus, *we must make sure the other person is as committed as we are!*

It's actually a tug of war for love! Little by little, we unleash our care and concern to another person in order to learn their character and weaknesses. All in all, the true reciprocation of love is required. If love isn't reciprocated, it means we are in a one-way love affair, and our mate will never be as committed as us.

### You're getting married... Why?

Most unmarried people still hope for marriage before "everything stops working." Haphazard selection of a mate due to loneliness, insecurity, or money problems can readily set up a relationship for a nuclear explosion.

The fear of turning thirty without a husband for a female is a devastating blow to a girl who wants a family. When a guy reaches forty who wanted a family and hasn't been married yet, he feels like a loser. While these emotions are being released, you also hear how divorce is raging out of control! You hear how single parent homes are the norm instead of the exception. Yet, the desire to marry is still extreme. Most people say they want a life-long companion and never want to be divorced, but that isn't happening at all.

Is it wise to marry quickly because a woman feels her time clock is running out, a man's libido is withering away, or because we finally decided if we don't marry this particular person, we'll never find another? Contentment would be a virtue at this point!

Years ago, there were statistics given for why people marry in the U.S. I recall 52% married for money, and 5% for love. Looking at divorce rates today, it's easy to believe. Love needs to be much greater than 5% in order to see divorce rates less than 50%. People are marrying for the wrong reasons! Motives need to be evaluated more seriously.

People marry for all sorts of reasons besides money or love. Some marry due to pre-marital pregnancies, desperation, or power. Some because the parents set it up, or just to spite a family member. Other times, people marry due to threats from the one they're dating. That would be something like, "I am going to kill myself if I lose you," or "You'll never find anybody like me again." Yes, these people hurt, but it's selfish for them to say.

In our hearts, we truly don't want to be with these people. Unfortunately, our minds race through some consequences that might evolve if we did walk away. If we walk, guilt stems because of the unfair pressure our beloved placed upon us. This insanity is created due to insecurities the other person possesses. At this point, we need a really good friend or family member to lean on, because this marriage will probably not last.

Sometimes, we see very pretty women or handsome men with unattractive mates. Usually, other people will make a comment about these "mismatches." Perhaps some of these relationships work, but most of them seem to send a powerful message of rebellion.

For the most part, the attractive person is the one rebelling. In essence, they hold the "power to capture whoever they want." If they pursue someone less appealing physically, their new mate is in "seventh heaven" because they cannot believe the "hunk" or "babe" they have on their arm! This may have transpired because the attractive person felt rejected quite often by other attractive people in dating or from a previous marriage. Many times I have heard people remark after a divorce, "the next time, I'm not going after love or looks, I'm going after the money!" This should say it all.

In many instances, a never married person may receive criticism or judgments from others who don't even know their name. The single may be an awesome person with much to give, but they are categorized because of the hurt so many others carry. Men and women will end up single because they won't settle for anything less than their "fantasy."

After my dad passed away, I took a deep look into his life. I went back to December 7, 1941 at Pearl Harbor. Remember, he could not swim, fought in seventeen battle zones, saw many of his buddies die, and came close with death innumerable times? This man, in all actuality, should have never made it out alive.

Do you know what? He returned without a physical scar. He built a business and ended up married with seven children. The moral is: *if something is meant to be, it will surely be!* There is a plan for us! If we are meant to be married, we'll surely be married! If we're meant to be single, then something beyond our imagination will happen designed specifically for us! There's only one catch. *God must be first in hierarchal priority!*

## A good woman's Advice
I heard a twenty-six year old woman say something that was so soothing that I have to share it. She said, "I want to be the wife and life-long girlfriend to my husband."

This statement is refreshing and steeped with magnetism toward the opposite sex. This woman triggered remarkable revelations in me about wanting to be married.

She wanted to be a _wife_ to someone. She didn't say she wanted to be _married_ to someone! Saying, "I want to be married," what does it mean? It depends upon the person!

Saying we want to be married might mean, "What can I, or the other person, get out of this arrangement from one another? A bigger bank account, golf course privileges, an open marriage, fifty percent of what he or she owns?" It's a selfish, self-centered and an insecure statement. It defines nothing about our purpose for being married!

On the other hand, knowing a woman wants to be a *wife,* all I heard was *commitment* and the first thing I felt was *warmth!* I knew her reason and purpose to marry.

The statement, "I want to be married," needs to be replaced with words of purpose. God intended for a woman to have the desire to be the wife and life-long girlfriend to her husband, and a man should have the desire to be the husband and life-long boyfriend to his wife!

Without doubt, my parents married with this goal. I never realized this so profoundly until I heard this woman's statement. More or less, I always took being married for granted, like so many other things in life. My parents both wanted children; they wanted to pursue their roles as husband and wife and as mother and father, girlfriend and boyfriend.

They always had their kids' best interests in front of them with the sacrifices they made. At the same time, they didn't spoil their children by giving them everything they wanted. They gave one thing they knew called love.

Today, it's reversed. Many parents give everything to their kids *except* a healthy form of love. These kids are future victims of spoiled relationships because they've never witnessed self-sacrifice, commitment, or love in action. This is mostly because people just want to be married.

## Marriage & dying to the World

When transitions occur from singleness to dating, dating to engagement and engagement to marriage, there should be significant differences in the relationship at each level. In singleness, it is all about me. While dating, center stage no longer belongs to me, and relationship is learned. In engagement, the decision to commit to someone for life is being rehearsed. However, in marriage, dying to the world is imperative for both people.

What on earth is "dying to the world?" Well, it's the number one thing no one wants to do, but everyone desperately needs to do in marriage. Couples contemplating marriage should focus on this concept intensely. It might scare them away from it. If you're currently married, it may literally save your marriage.

Everyone knows the definition of commitment... it's something men never do! That's about the depth of that subject to many. Please help us! Anyway, now that I have your attention, the concept of "dying to the world" needs to be explained. It will actually help intensify mutual commitment.

Christian wisdom emphasizes that a man should love his wife as Christ loved the church. How did He love the church (His children)? If you've read about it, He suffered and died for it (us). So guys, we need to *suffer* and *die* for our wives or our future wives!

Have you ever heard some married men say, "I suffer for all I put up with and wish to die because I want to?" I don't think this is what Christ meant!

I used to think I would literally die for my wife. I'd picture jumping in front of a bullet coming her way; I'd walk on the street side of the sidewalk so if a car ran the curb, it would take me out before her, or whatever else could be conjured up!

As time passed, I realized there aren't many bullets flying by a man's wife, and there isn't much walking going on anymore except in malls! So, I started thinking about dying to the world differently, and by golly, it makes a little bit more sense.

Authentically "dying to the world" is much harder than taking a bullet or physically dying for our wives, even though that could be the case. "Dying to the world" means *eliminating* single events that used to surround us; it's *eliminating* lusts, pornography, talking about other women, looking at other women, putting our golf game to the side to be with our wife, or *eliminating* any other habits we have that don't nurture the relationship!

As mentioned in Chapter 8, this is the bridge that links a man's number one hierarchal priority (God) to his next priority (wife) by exposing this kind of love to her. It makes her feel secure knowing that a man isn't "looking elsewhere." In return, she respects, honors, and submits to her godly husband.

Please understand that a guy shouldn't have to forfeit golf, hunting or fishing the rest of his life. He needs his *space*, as does his wife. I am saying his *priorities have changed.*

It seems that when people marry, they still try to keep up the single life when they are no longer a part of it. We have now chosen the person we want to be with, and we must sleep with him or her in our beds forever more!

# Chapter 21

## To Pursue or Not To Pursue

Men pursue what they feel is sexy or attractive in a female. She's the initial recipient of a guy's invitation to allow a one on one rendezvous. She either accepts or rejects his offer based on her wants. That is normal and how things used to work. No other complications were involved to hinder a prospective date.

Nowadays, a man might be reluctant to pursue a woman for a relationship because of unknown expectations and the pressures associated with it. Rejection can be delivered to him by simply trying to strike up small talk. It's from this point he discovers her attitude and/or entitlement combo. Nonetheless, these same women log-on to a computer to find true love! Men log-on to their computers to feel they are innately pursuing... via email.

If a man attempts to ask a woman on a date, he is acting out his roles of hunter and pursuer. She doesn't know how long it took him to muster up his courage to ask. Her only task would be to let him know if she is interested or not. If he is sincere, it's kind for a woman to grant him a brief moment, and respond with an appropriate answer. This helps him overcome any fear of rejection he may be struggling with, and makes it safe to approach other women if she is not interested in his company.

A woman might *approach* a man if she thinks he is shy, or confused of her situation. Men welcome this because they're not standing at the door of rejection. However, *she is not to try and pursue him!* There's a huge difference between *approaching* a guy because of an interest, and *pursuing* him into a relationship. *He'll pursue if he is interested!*

A man is flattered, just as a woman, if she compliments him, or initially strikes up small talk. She may be crazy over this guy, and ends up exhibiting too much pressure in order to "capture" him. He may become uncomfortable because he's unable to pursue. If she pursues, it pushes him away emotionally, but physically he's still there.

If she unknowingly pushes him away, his emotions diffuse. His interest to connect passionately lasts only momentarily. A man's emotions are tied to his pursuit! If a female invades that area, good luck in long-term success. When a man feels pursued, he discovers his part in choosing a mate has no merit, he feels a loss of respect, and that he'll never end up with his "dream girl." His "fake ego" comes into play, and he questions his dignity as a man.

A man may stick around because of an existing mutual friendship. It's a tough spot to be in. He may not want to lose a friend, or hurt her feelings. She has shown a strong desire to be with him, even though the level of friendship has been previously discussed.

Further down the road, it becomes more difficult for both to let go. He considers she's a nice girl, but one he never pursued. He permitted his passivity to operate and allowed things to continue. This occurred because he never considered her as his "dream girl." As for her, she has become more attached emotionally.

If she's unaware of all of this, she may pursue more aggressively because he hasn't communicated his true feelings. In the meanwhile, she's saying things he likes to hear in order for her to become more desirable. She may also disclose things that concern him regarding her "time clock," and motherly desires. Most likely, he'll become standoffish.

Finally, *her* pursuit wins him. They become an "item" and everything seems great at first. After a few weeks or months, he becomes frustrated with how things formulated. At last, the reality of her pursuit and his passivity collide. He now sees how damaging his passivity was because he never put his "stamp of approval" on the matter. He also realizes how he allowed this nice girl to utilize her masculine side more than he used his.

Even though this may have transpired, they get married! Unless this guy really grew to love her, he may start *pursuing* other women in his marriage. Subconsciously, his need to pursue hasn't been fulfilled. Along with it, he may become passive/aggressive, have an affair, or experience separation leading to a divorce.

Hopefully, this enactment will assist us in understanding the power of our innate functions. They are real and should never be pushed aside because we have an opportunity to conquer something beyond our reach. If we'll just accept how we were innately created to operate, there would be plenty of men and women to go around!

## Electronic Compatibility

We are taught to seek out our *"soul-mates."* Actually, God created *"helpmates"* for us to seek out. If our souls are composed of our mind, will, and emotions, how do we find our *"mind, will, and emotions-mate?"* I don't think we can. Maybe it's why they're hard to find! Ideally, we need to find a godly man or woman who will *help* us to enjoy the good times and *help* us to get through the bad times in life. Later on, we'll think alike, act alike, and love at deeper levels. Over time is when I believe we become *"soul-mates."*

Nonetheless, we go online to seek a person with common interests, from hobbies we enjoy, to where we like to live. Even though we diligently search out love, we experience constant rejection that leads to fear, failure, depression or other negative emotions. Maybe, if we rid ourselves of attitudes and entitlements, God could go to work for us, and create a meeting with a person for us to experience the "real thing!"

Many females say, "You don't know who anyone is anymore. There are a lot of weirdoes out there!" So, everyone gets treated like one? Are they saying dating sites consist of fewer weirdoes? I believe there's more emotional and mental harm done to a person on an electronic dating site than if you met someone face to face.

Meeting someone in person, we *see* the real deal, we *feel* the real deal. If a guy truly wants to be with someone, he'll insist on a date. Healthy chemistry is either there or it isn't. If it's there, we experience an excitement; if it isn't there, we politely bow out.

We're so busy today, there's hardly a chance for chemistry to work face to face. So, when we get a minute, the computer, with all its glory, is turned on to find the love of our lives. Pictures are scrolled and excitement builds over a photo. The picture is perfect and the essays say everything we want to hear. There's so much commonality, it's a miracle, or is it lust?

The excitement, dreams and expectations begin to build. We spend a measly twenty-five dollars to "connect" with a potential mate. Confidence is high, knowing without a doubt, they're anxiously waiting for a reply with our picture and profile they cannot resist!

We continue checking our email to see if Prince Charming or Miss Right has replied. A day, two days, or a week passes with no response. A little frustration builds because he or she was perfect for us! Then, we rationalize, the person must have found someone else, or they left the site. After we experience some anger or rejection for a short while, and the initial shock wears off, we log on again to find our next new e-love!

Finally, there's a connection with someone who takes an interest in us. Conversations on the phone begin as we visualize the person from the photo they emailed. Everything is great and a meeting is scheduled. The time arrives to meet as we nervously anticipate the presence of healthy interest. Even though hours and hours may be spent on the phone or computer with this person, we still don't know if sparks will fly!

Nonetheless, we recognize we've been stood up because the other person was staked out to get a glimpse of the truth! Or, if we do meet, it's hard to ignore the fact that the person's picture was from a decade ago. Maybe it really wasn't them in the first place! If we keep our composure, we talk over a drink and learn their age is off a little, or that they're married. Look at all the time we've wasted to know someone we don't like!

A popular news program had a report on Internet Dating in July of 2004. Some statistics were amazing. They reported that there are 90 million singles in America. They didn't give the age range of these singles and whether they were divorced or not. On a monthly basis, 40 million people log-on to these sites! In 2003, it was a 400 million dollar industry! Holy desperate relationships Batman!

See what our measly twenty-five dollars will do? It makes someone very rich off our emotions. What a great business venture to jump into if we don't mind hurting people. With all the logging on, how many people are mentally unstable, or trying to defile children? How many are looking for multiple partners? How many are bored at home with nothing to do and need a pen pal? How many men and women are cheating on their spouses? I am sure the list continues.

Another tale behind Internet Dating is the *delusion* most people have in finding their spouse. There's an extremely high rate of divorce out there. People are trying to find someone before they begin a healing process. In essence, people hide behind the computer with hurt feelings, and try to communicate their best side.

In reality, most people's experiences have left them more lonely and frustrated. The natural progression of meeting the opposite sex has been annihilated. Thus, the games some men and women play on the computer might lead them to the next fantasy. This "fulfillment" comes with another click of the button to some great porn site!

This is the most authentic sensation received. After a little of this, they're able to move on with their life until the next temptation of meeting their *"soul-mate"* in cyberspace percolates. Many times the whole thing becomes a pit to throw our money into, and we become more desensitized in the proper process of building relationship intimacy.

I calculated the success of meeting a person and

getting married from one popular dating site. It has a multi-million person membership. From the millions of members, I calculated 1/10th of one percent of success! That's rather low for all the psychology and investment of hope, don't you think? I'm sure our chances at a bar would be just as good!

## Picture Perfect?

If I log onto a dating site, I need my visual *first*. Most women like to see a picture too, and they aren't as visual. We can be compatible with someone blindly, but when the visual test comes, an incompatible situation may arise. For those needing a visual, how do they know a person's size, appearance, or race? They may have stated all of this in their essay, but things are different by sight.

Going through these dating sites and noticing the number of people that don't post pictures after their subscription, you have to wonder many things. Is this person really ugly, are they married, are men or women on the wrong side of the site, or is this person a professional e-dater or spy? Who knows what's going on?

We also need to be aware of those who confiscate pictures of handsome men, or beautiful women from around the world. We may fall in love with what they say in their emails. At some point, our heart breaks after our money was confiscated! It is hard to tell who's really on the other side of a computer.

So far, Internet dating seems much riskier than just being friendly on the street, in the store, at work, or wherever you may be. Remember, we were told that technology would make our lives much easier many years ago!

# Chapter 22

## Pounding Hearts & Pounding Minds

The sub-section titled, *"The Sea of Confusion,"* in Chapter 2, reflects the difference in the dating scene before I went overseas, and what it was like after I returned home from the Navy. I was in disbelief, as it delivered a sharp pounding to my heart and mind. There was a sudden progressive change regarding relationships.

An example of this type of change can be found at the gas pump. Remember when gas was $1.30 per gallon? Then it was $1.60, $1.90 and then $2.40 or more? When we first saw the price increases we were in disbelief. People understood prices might go up, but not that drastically. Once the initial shock wore off, we got used to paying higher prices, but have we ever really accepted them?

Well, progressive change has happened in society regarding morals and values. It seemed that people got along fairly well wherever they went until the 1980's arrived. Nonetheless, some issues were pending in the 1960's that needed attention. We experienced an onslaught of social issues, and our hearts and minds pounded at first because of the amount of changes taking place.

Many of the changes were desperately needed. However, we have constantly paid higher prices for our sexual freedom, the choice to abort, working mothers, cohabitation, and no-fault divorce, etc. After the initial shock wore off in the 60's, no one thought the changes would have been this drastic. But, have we ever really accepted them?

I'm hopeful after hearing a news report that talked about a survey given to British women, whose ages ranged from their late teens to their mid twenties. A very high percentage of these women were rebelling against the single-parent homes in which they were raised. They have started to demand hugs from their men. They desire life-long relationship in a traditional family setting, and for sex to be a matrimonial gift!

Oh my goodness, what an awesome pounding of the heart and mind. What a wonderful step forward as they unleash the *"Power of a Woman!"* If they corporately stick together with their *power* and *self-control*, they'll win their hugs, love, commitment and respect from men. At the same time, pornography will be reduced as marriages increase with strength, abortion rates will drop, and venereal disease and violent crimes will become less widespread.

I'm aware every person's marital issue won't be solved because of this step. For the most part, a *tolerable* number of divorces will return to the playing field. A vast decrease in divorce is what we want, and it's what our communities need!

### Realizing hurt in the heart and Soul

The greatest hell on earth a person can experience, in my opinion, is taking a glimpse at the lies, resentments, bitterness, hurts, and anger they have carried out so well, for so long. It requires courage to face our own mind, will and emotions, collectively known as our *soul*. Lives become vividly different once we begin to heal our hurts.

Many people run from their own soul. It's been programmed so long with rejection and negative statements, it's easier to operate under those pessimistic influences than to dig in and fight against them. Consequently, relationships, prospective relationships, jobs, prosperity, and peace are all robbed. We blame others for our own problems, and end up single, divorced, and bankrupt, or plastered with fake body parts and tattoos.

It's easier to file a lawsuit and blame someone else than to admit fault and grant forgiveness. A person's pain is so great, their heart and soul are hardened. This hardness is a total defense mechanism allowing no filtration of love, gentleness or kindness to *act*. Everything in life, with all of its trials, receives a *reaction*.

Nevertheless, the question needing to be answered is, "Are my heart and soul healthy enough to *act* upon life's twists and turns, or are my *reactions* volatile enough to destroy my dreams and everything around me?"

As time slipped by with no prospects for life-long companionship, I started thinking about the emotions that dwelt within males and females. After my own healing initiated, I began to look into people's hearts and souls from a distance, and felt the pain they often hid from others. I saw these individuals saying and doing things that were damaging to them, and how these things affected their prosperity and relationships. Their *words* and *actions* were the avenues used to hide the hurt and pain deep within them. It's now so common it has become "normal."

Take for example, a "macho" man with walls built around his heart and soul. Due to the injury of these precious components, ranging from dysfunctional parenting to female rejection, he feels the need to perform at an optimum level. No matter what he attempts, failure arises. Initially he would *act* in a situation, but after all the hurts, he starts to *react* in order to be heard. His wounded heart and soul leads to violence in a relationship and in society.

People using foul language think they are "cool." They often believe their "coolness' is a road to acceptance, or it demonstrates how mad they are, as they reach out and try to connect with another. This mentality believes there is substantial power behind their opinion, when in reality they scare off the person they're speaking to.

This type of language is a defense mechanism that is actually *uncovering* their hurts. They want to express their inner pain and get it off their chest, but they already believe their opinion won't be heard. Thus, intense yelling, language, and unacceptable behavior formulate.

I found myself empathizing with more women. I constantly tried to figure out why a lot of female personalities were so tainted. This is when I began to see women's most significant gifts of kindness, fun-lovingness, innocence, sweetness, and their nurturing abilities tarnished. Their dreams in their hearts, and the programming of their souls, showed me men's contributions to their pain. I saw the pattern of destruction regarding femininity and masculinity.

All of this pain we carry is very deep. We hurt loved ones or acquaintances without realizing it. A person's hardened heart says he or she doesn't need you, or anyone else. This person continues to distance themselves from everyone, until complete disharmony is achieved. These are the type of things I started to notice once my hurts began to heal.

### Conflict of heart and Soul
Like many, my desire for life-long relationship burned daily. I realized how soiled my own heart and soul

were. The desires on my insides were for wine and roses. My outsides were always in some sort of conflict, unable to buy either of them!

Then it hit me. My heart and soul were in constant conflict with each other. There was no peace inside, as a spiritual war was raging on between "good and evil" or "right and wrong." It also meant other people saw things on my outsides I never could. You or I may act like a devil, and that was never embarrassing to us! Try talking to someone about your pain… that's embarrassing! Aren't we ridiculous and strange creatures?

We think of how romantic, loving, and close our relationships would be with the "perfect girl or guy." Our mind races in front of our heart because of loneliness or insecurities. Initially, we try to impress someone by *depositing* everything we have to offer relationally. Later, we try to *withdraw* everything from the other person until they are emotionally bankrupt!

Nonetheless, our mind created a perfect relationship. We mentally rehearsed everything we would say and do. As soon we arrive with the flowers, everything goes the opposite way of what was envisioned! It seems never ending. Maybe we can unravel this tormenting conflict before going any further.

### Gentle hearts, renewed Minds
Have you ever regretted anything you've said or done, wishing it never happened? This may be an act of a hardened heart. There's a lack of control over words and actions. The mind thinks positively of how great things could be, but the heart is the instrument leading us to say or do the very thing we didn't want to happen. *"You brood of vipers, how can you who are evil say anything good? For out of the overflow of*

*the heart the mouth speaks"* (Mat 12:34).

The heart is the explosive part of our being, and bypasses the mind if it's in turmoil. Thoughts and actions come from our heart. *"For out of the heart come evil thoughts, murder, adultery, sexual immorality, theft, false testimony and slander"* (Mat 15:19). Our thoughts need to be filtered in our minds before words are spoken, or an action taken.

Maybe we've never heard or realized the things we say. Nevertheless, this is why it's difficult to bite our tongue in any relational conflict! All the hurt in our spirit is riled. Our defenses go up, walls go up, and another person receives all sorts of physical, mental and/or emotional injury. In turn, their heart and mind is broken.

Our hearts, *spirits,* should be gentle, so that good thoughts are sent to our minds. Our minds need to be renewed, in order for thoughts to be processed before we speak. When we become whole in mind and spirit, we won't feel "attacked" or rejected by someone else's insecurity. Our choice of a mate will be sane. Our commitment will be life-long, and over time, all sorts of prosperity will be reaped.

Infomercials try to sell us audio tapes that deliver subliminal messages. The intent is to have them "rewrite" our "hard-drives" by listening to them over and over. In turn, our human strength strives to eradicate our old thinking patterns and behaviors. The tapes are unable to touch our spirits. We might experience a brief moment of relief. However, if our hearts aren't changed first, our explosive nature will erupt when tested again.

Do you want a zero percent divorce rate in your life? Do you want to experience peace, and have the dark hole in your chest filled with life? I guarantee that drugs, alcohol, sex, money, chanting to ungodly spirits, and all the rest will not work.

There is only *one universal* answer to our problems. *Renewal must start in our heart by requesting God's presence.* Once we accept this fact, gentle hearts and soft minds will develop as God's Spirit sensitizes our conscience. It is this power that renews our mind with lasting effects!

*"The mind of sinful man is death, but the mind controlled by the spirit is life and peace; the sinful mind is hostile to God. It does not submit to God's law, nor can it do so. Those controlled by the sinful nature cannot please God. You, however, are controlled not by the sinful nature but by the spirit, if the spirit of God lives in you..."* (Rom 8:6-9).

Having a soft heart is not being passive, having no opinions, or showing signs of weakness. A soft heart brings back masculinity, femininity, and the innate roles we were intended to carry out. It allows us to speak the truth in love. Both genders have *equal opportunity* to receive such virtues!

# Chapter 23

# The Greatest Lie of All Time

Since the days of the Sexual Revolution, Equal Opportunity, and all the rest, many precious women have been blatantly lied to. They were told they could "*do it all.*" If this is true, why then, are heart attacks among women their number one death threat? I don't think it's the food they eat and the lack of exercise, even though it's vital to heart health. Why *is it* they eat badly and avoid exercise?

With many women, the *reasons* for their heart attacks are kept secret. It would be embarrassing to admit the real source. Instinctive reasoning tells me they're under horrific stress because they're trying to do it all! They have no time to eat healthy, exercise, nurture themselves properly during monthly cycles, or receive the love they desire. We could probably all agree that enormous stress is the root of the problem.

"*Women can do it all*" is the lie I am discussing. The interpretation many have believed is, "I can get married, have children, get a job, higher education, cook the meals, clean the house, get the laundry done, travel for business, take care of my husband, the pets, and anything else that needs to be done because I am woman and I can now do it all!" This is actually called Third Wave Feminism. Old feminism, new problems!

This does not reflect the characteristics of the proverbial woman that are stated in Proverbs 31:10-31. The proverbial woman does work, make money, and have a family in order to assist her husband and help the needy. He receives respect not only at home, but outside of it because of her. Her children are taken care of, and they rejoice in her. The proverbial woman is free from shame, disgrace, anxiety and worry. Her husband praises her!

I personally don't know anyone, of either gender, who can do it all, and do it *successfully*. Take myself for example. I have a remodeling business to run. Simultaneously, I pursued to write this book. In the beginning, I started to write at 10:00 p.m., and continued until 3:00 a.m. This went on quite often for twelve months. Once I sat to read the book, I knew I had to stop working and focus on it! So, I didn't work, or go on vacation for almost five months. I put an average of 14 hours a day behind the project because I believed in it wholeheartedly.

The point is ladies; you've been given *freedom* to make a *choice* of what to do with your lives. No longer do you have to marry for financial reasons, take care of the house, the kids or a husband. You are now are able to *choose* to be the wife of a good man *or* remain single and have a full time career. You can travel as deemed necessary *or* be a missionary overseas. You can be in politics *or* whatever else your heart desires. Trying to *do it all at once* may harm you or other significant people.

## Making your Choice

Most people have opportunity and a *choice* to do what they want, especially in the United States. Usually, God has a calling or plan for what He wants us to do. Many can't hear His direction because of all the noise and turmoil surrounding them.

Do you have a natural talent attaining higher results than those with a degree? Do you have insight for the masses? Is there an exceptional understanding of electronics, healthcare, or childrearing? This type of person wonders why

214

schooling is necessary. In some cases it sharpens our *God-given* abilities. Mostly, it's to prove our qualifications.

Consequences are attached by going outside of our God-given abilities. It often affects our health, relationships, and pocketbooks. We should pursue our talents no matter if it's engineering, secretarial work, being a mother or father, a salesperson, or whatever. If we want to change careers, houses, or a goal, that is great... however, *our mate is for life!*

Trying to accomplish everything simultaneously and expecting victory in every area is ludicrous. Men have achieved an average of three things at once. They'd get married, have a family and go to work, *or* remain single, work and explore the world. It's a *choice.*

Nonetheless, being a wife is a huge job, and an extremely important one at that. She's an *extension* of her husband. Being a homemaker is more important than trying to hold down a career. Being home with the children is the right choice. Something will bust if everything's attempted in unison, and it won't be the career!

Our culture has proclaimed to women that it's easier to work in corporate America rather than staying home to raise the kids. It has been said that raising a family is twice as much work! Many women feel they're contributing more profoundly in the workplace rather than "just raising a family." Consequently, many children pay the price.

## Absolute Equality

Everywhere I've lived, heated discussions arise about the meaning of "equality." I found the false version can be interpreted in as many ways as there are individuals. However, absolute equality was established by our Creator.

215

"Equality," in my experiences, began with the notion of sexual freedom, and traveled all the way to a woman being able to "*do it all*." In actuality, arguments regarding equality came down to "equal pay for equal work." With this, there's no argument left. It's a no-brainer! Equal pay should be received by both genders who work the same job, if similar knowledge and experience are brought to the table.

I am stuck in a paradox, nonetheless. Most of the women I know make more money than the men I know. There are instances that arise due to unfairness. However, it seems a lot of women are more interested in fighting for equal pay than fighting for their family.

Equal pay is a woman's *right*. So, what is absolute equality? It isn't being able to do anything a man can do, or having the same privileges of his gender. This equality is a God given virtue given at birth. Both genders were created equally in the image of God, with mind, body, spirit, will and emotions. *Both sexes have the same exact individual opportunity to abide by spiritual laws and have a free choice of eternal destiny.* In the end, it doesn't matter if you were a doctor, nurse, mother, father, secretary, or whatever. What matters is that you performed your duties with integrity, character, and godliness!

*If we think about equality in real terms, it allows our own free will, awarded to us by our Creator, to make rational decisions within the boundaries of our own gender. The decisions we make are in direct relation to the roles we were assigned from the beginning, as a man or a woman.*

Men and women have *equal opportunity* lying right in front of them. Their decision to be honorable, to love their neighbor, to respect and honor those in the position to receive it, to pursue what is good, to love and to submit to others; these virtues are all equally accessible. Once again, femininity, masculinity, morals and roles are our *choice*.

### The lack of relational Education

Every generation, since the beginning of mankind, has always had problems with gender issues, equal opportunity, and relationship. The battle of the sexes began when Eve blamed the serpent, and Adam blamed Eve for disobeying God. Adam was a passive leader. He neglected his assigned role of headship, which was supposed to ensure that he and his *helpmate* obeyed God.

Adam wasn't educated in knowing how to have relationship with Eve and vice versa. She was thrown right into his life! Relationship was completely new to them. They had no formal education or previous relationships to lean on for guidance. They actually designed the relationship prototype!

This trend has continued until present day. There's no mandatory classroom study on successful life-long relationships. However, there are sex education classes for children that their parents should be involved with. Teaching a child about the "birds and the bees" at home is where this should take place. Nonetheless, preteens receive their information from misinformed sources.

Ignoring sex education in the home today is dangerous. Parents should open up and prepare their children, before some anonymous radical permeates their mind. If parents fear the subject, or think their child is too young to understand, they know best. Otherwise, I think it's time to wake up and smell the coffee! The subject on the streets, or in the schools, is all about sex and inappropriate language. Mom or dad need to plant the first seeds of truth, before radical influence does!

In other words, dad, step up to the plate with boldness, passion and assertiveness regarding premarital sex with your daughters. Talk to them and your sons about things they need to understand before they misinterpret their meanings. It's better to lay down the law, than to see a child pregnant with a child!

Schools have condoms available for teenagers, as do pregnancy clinics. So, instead of instilling good morals into our kids, we insist on being passive with the most sacred subject regarding life. If something goes astray, we start blaming everyone around us.

The only relational education we've ever had, is watching our parents relate to each other, and allowing our hormones to connect us with the opposite sex. We play "spin the bottle," and then we're professionals on how to handle a marriage. Unfortunately, many children today don't have two parents under the same roof in order to even witness good relationship. They're only familiar with heartbreak, and don't know anything different.

We all know it starts with our parents for us to inherit good morals, character and values. Many kids are pawned off into society emotionally crippled and pay the consequences dearly. Then, they become adults.

A myriad of inner healing needs to be accomplished before marriage can be thought of. Nonetheless, the amount of hurt, rejection, guilt, fear, shame, and abuse of all sorts, has us hiding within ourselves, or exploding on others. We make bad decisions due to extremely poor judgment, ungodly guidance, and *the lack of relational education.*

## Divine guidance Systems

God has given us two sources of guidance systems. One is our "gut feeling" and the other is our conscience. How many times have we said to ourselves, "I should have listened to my gut?" Sometimes the gut is the source of intuition, and other times our conscience may bother us if we try doing something ill-mannered. Many times we ignore it because we may not think the thought was valid because it came and went so fast.

I wonder how many couples have approached the altar with a huge "gut ache!" Their stomach is churning away, and it's often passed off for nerves. Elsewhere in the body, voices prompt people to go forward with the ceremony, while their conscience bothers them. Other times, drugs or alcohol have smothered our guidance systems as we seek the proper direction to take in our lives.

Butterflies are different than churning stomachs! A churning stomach is a divine guidance system saying, "Do not do this!" Butterflies announce a positive change in life. A conscience that isn't warring against an action we are about to take is what we seek. If peace isn't present in our mind, we are probably making the wrong decision.

Sometimes we may hear comments about people being guided through life. It comes across as magic, or as being a puppet on a string. God won't come down out of the heavens, and steer us right or left, nor are there any puppet strings to make us move in a certain direction. We need to heed to our *"divine guidance systems!"*

There are several indicators of knowing if we made a sane and rational decision. *It's all within our body.* No matter what decision we're trying to make, from buying a car, a

219

house, or wanting to marry, remember, we'll be at peace with the right decision. If any stress is evident physically, emotionally, spiritually or mentally, we're most likely headed down the wrong avenue. No *significant* amounts of stress should exist in any one of these areas while finalizing our choice.

I like to make decisions using my stress indicators. If they are ignored, life keeps moving forward with some friction. This internal friction may create a little more heat than the previous day. Before we know it, we're burning up, life explodes, and we end up back at the starting line. We continue to go through the same cycle several times until we realize our gut was saying something different, or that our conscience was not at peace.

Unfortunately, we live in a high stress society. Broken marriages, multiple jobs, neglected children, temptations, and sin are present wherever we go. People swallow pain so deeply that God's divine guidance systems are annulled. Too many problems are stacked on top of "His voice."

Without gentle hearts and renewed minds, our own will shall guide us down the path of no return. It's imperative to have a personal relationship with God, in order to sensitize our conscience, and to be able to distinguish butterflies from churning stomachs.

# Before the Finale

We've surely been through a lot together. We started out with my parents who had fifty-three years of marriage, and then traveled through many obstacles preventing such success. We talked about spiritual side effects, and got to the root of the decay in our families and communities. We saw how Satan's scheme is to destroy, shatter, and ruin our hopes, dreams, and eternal destiny. We opened the door of resolve with God, confession, forgiveness, and for eternal living. We have discovered *"Why Singles are not Married & the Married are Single"* by getting to the hearts of many individuals.

In summarizing this work, I am saddened by the men who have neglected their roles and their family, and who are consciously using women sexually. I am proud of the men who have served this nation to give us the freedoms we enjoy, and who love their wives and children. I am ashamed of some men because of the bad rap they've given the good ones, and the selfishness they possess. Men are supposed to be leaders, and much appreciation goes to the men who acknowledge their duties and responsibilities and who are creating strong families.

I'm saddened by the women who have neglected their roles by using the power God gave them in an ungodly manner, and who are using men sexually to gain the wrong type of power and position. I am proud of the women who do their everyday best to balance the heavy load of single parenthood, and who are sticking to roles in a world that doesn't appreciate them. I am ashamed of the women who constantly try to invade men's space, and try to prove that they are "better" than a man. Women are a powerful influence to a man, and I appreciate every one of you who have been misled, abused, taken for granted, lied to, and have taken the time to read this book.

God's gift of relationship is His perfect desire for us. Unfortunately, we have perfected imperfection since Adam and Eve. So now, let's open a new chapter and unveil a pattern that may help explain the road well traveled.

# Regarding Chapters One & Two

Let's take a moment to draw a more profound parallel between Adam and Eve and the problems they faced in the Garden of Eden with the problems we face today in our own lives and relationships.

In Chapter One of Genesis, Moses disclosed God's accomplishments of His "sixth day" creation. *"So God created man in his own image, in the image of God he created him; male and female he created them"* (Gen 1:27). Thus, before Adam's creation, no one ever emulated the image of God. Conceivably, if any other people were walking the earth prior to Adam, they were not worthy of honor and respect, they didn't have the ability to be righteous, holy or knowledgeable! Choice, morality, servant-hood and kingship became available to Adam and to all who followed. Animals were also created in the "sixth day." They never assumed God's image. Strength was, and is, their only virtue.

Chapter Two of Genesis magnifies the "sixth day" creation of man. It seems that Adam was single a long time before he had a mate. His assignment in his singleness was to work the Garden and to name all the creatures of the earth. Eve arrived *after* Adam completed God's work. Since we don't know how long a day was, Eve may have appeared in that "sixth day," a month, a year, or a decade down the road in retrospect to our time-line. *"But do not forget this one thing, dear friends: With the Lord a day is like a thousand years and a thousand years are like a day"* (2Peter 3:8).

Remember, God *gave* Adam his mate when *God* was ready, not when Adam thought he was ready! Eve was sexually pure and morally innocent when given to Adam. Her relational, feminine and nurturing abilities were not

223

tainted. She didn't pursue Adam. She was the ultimate gift from God for companionship. God determined the time and place for their meeting, not Adam. God's plan was perfect and right on time.

Are you single and find yourself without a mate in the "season of life" that you've been assigned? Have you completed the work God has prompted you to do? Are you acting like God in order to make things happen in your life rather than walking in His image, or are you impersonating an animal? Have you reserved any purity for your future husband or wife for life-long companionship, or have you allowed others to help destroy your innocence by observing their double standards?

### Following Rules
Life was good in Eden and God was pleased. The "tree of life" was available to eat from, which gave spiritual life! However, in order to keep harmony between man and God, one simple rule had to be followed. That was, *"not to eat from the tree of knowledge of good and evil."* Eating from that specific "tree" carried the consequence of spiritual death due to disobeying God's rule.

At one point, Eve had a conversation with the serpent (Satan). The serpent convinced Eve that she wouldn't die by eating "fruit from the forbidden tree." He told her, *"For God knows that when you eat of it your eyes will be opened, and you will be like God, knowing good and evil"* (Gen 3:5). Unfortunately, his delicious lie and temptation overcame Eve. Her choice was to eat of the fruit and be like God. She also gave some to Adam who was with her, and he also chose to eat of the fruit as stated in Genesis 3:6. Adam and Eve had free choice just like you and I have every day.

What went wrong? Adam was the leader and responsible to God in his hierarchical priority. Why did he accept the fruit instead of correct the situation? He knew what God told him. Why would he partake of this particular fruit with Eve with so many others available? I believe we see the first instance of passivity in a man and control in a woman surface! Because Adam was passive towards God, and Eve wasn't submissive, devastating problems occurred, and a *consequence* had to be paid.

The consequence was spiritual death. Adam and Eve were immortal prior to their disobedience; now they became mortal man and woman. They went from eternal living to earthly lives. That's pretty substantial for only biting into an "apple" never mentioned!

Has passivity or control brought substantial consequences to your life through disobedience to God? What conversation are you having with Satan that can destroy life around you or in you? Is it leading to spiritual death? Is it obvious that *both* genders contribute to adultery, divorce, cohabitation, abortion, pornography and all the rest? What choices are you making to help create disharmony in your life and in the lives of those that you love?

God placed rules in the Garden of Eden for the well-being of ancient man. He places rules in our lives because He wants us to avoid the consequences of sin! He loves us and knows the depth of the hurt, pain, and suffering that may occur. That's all. Unfortunately, we usually ignore the laws of protection and end up in misery.

## But the fruit was so Tempting!
*"Then the eyes of both of them were opened, and they realized they were naked; ..."* (Gen 3:7-7n). Adam

and Eve had felt no shame in their nakedness (innocence) before choosing to challenge God. Can you imagine being totally naked in front of someone and never realizing it? It's extremely hard to grasp. Nonetheless, once the rules were broken, their eyes were "opened," they realized each others nakedness, and they hid in *shame*.

When have you felt the most shame? What specific incident occurred, where you wanted to crawl up into a hole and hide from God and yourself? Why is it, when this particular incident happens, you feel disconnected from God and fight to reconnect? I am sure that Adam and Eve wanted to reconnect with God after they sinned.

To feel shame is the result from an act, against our own selves, which makes us wish the episode never took place. It's something we can't shake off by just saying, "I'm sorry." It's deeper than that, takes time to get over, and settles into the core of our being.

Guilt is more of a mind game that plays with our emotions. We were caught doing something that may have injured another. We have to own up quickly or suffer within.

In my own case, I remember when I first challenged God. I was passive to His spiritual laws of protection. I realized that disobedience to God made me reap ill emotions as I hid in shame from Him and myself. His law states, *"not to eat from the tree of knowledge of good and evil."* This particular "tree" is always tempting and prepared with awesome fruit. The "fruit," I "bit" into happened to be... ***a woman's body.***

Is your ***"tree"*** either a man's body or a woman's body? Doesn't the sin of fornication, adultery, or homosexuality bring on **shame** and guilt simultaneously? Don't you want to run and **hide** from God after partaking of the *fruit*? Have you experienced the **good** part of sex for marital pleasure and to bear children, or have you experienced the *evil* part of sex that brings on abortion, venereal disease, or a physical death threat? Weren't your eyes **opened** deeply with a profound spiritual **knowledge** of your partner after sexual intimacy? Wasn't the relationship tainted, destroyed, or delayed with a person you truly cared about? Didn't arguments, disagreements, and power struggles occur after unsanctioned sex? Weren't respect, honor and submission toward your partner affected? Isn't this when your internal conflicts surfaced and you acted out of character?

Perhaps sexual sin is so rampant today because Satan has always known that it is the most powerful, tempting and enticing pleasure for men and women to restrain from before God's appointed time! This temptation does not discriminate against any gender, race, or creed, and has the power to separate us from God and His perfect plan. At the same time, it is the most destructive force Satan can utilize to shame mankind and to create misery amongst God's people. While talking to Eve in the garden, perhaps Satan knew man's eyes would be **opened**, and they would "be like God" because they would be enabled to **create life** as God did, but the avenue would be through sex, not omnipotence.

When a person or society "falls" it is usually instigated by lewd conduct. A "fall" can be initiated between two people who disregard God's law of sexual purity in singleness, monogamy in marriage, or by participating in homosexual acts. Ignoring sexual morals will result in shame as we try to hide from God. Our shame limits full participation in society as spiritually whole people. Our conscience becomes desensitized while our future of true prosperity is being impacted. Gloom engulfs us, confusing family, friends, and neighbors. Rational decision making is stifled and our hearts' desires are destroyed.

As this dilemma perpetuates from one couple to the next and becomes more widespread, people become less sensitive, more selfish and very unfriendly. The overall result leads to weakened families, communities and nations.

I feel a warning has been established to put sex back into marriage between heterosexual couples. We need to restrain from premarital sex, (yes, oral sex is sex) and be monogamous in heterosexual marriage. Our conscience will become more sensitive and the side effects of depression and all the rest will lessen. We will be more patient in waiting for God to give us our mate when He is ready, while we do the work He wants us to do in the "season of life" we are in.

# Final Thoughts

There's plenty to think about, if we choose to do so. We must determine our spiritual condition, which is directly proportional to the quality of life in our homes and community. We need to heed simple truths and morals. Otherwise, strife, grief, and bitterness will continue to get the best of us. When bad things happen in life, God is often to blame. We need to stop and look at what *we* are doing to create it! God has emotions, and He sits in a room of tears because of our choices.

There are the times God allows things to happen. He never stopped the suffering of His own Son. It's part of His divine plan, just as you and I are. We live in a thing called *life*. Nothing or no one is perfect, but we can at least try to *"Love our neighbor as ourselves."*

We have a choice as Adam and Eve did. We can choose the *"Tree of Life"* rooted in the eternal destiny of life and love, or *"The Tree of Knowledge of Good and Evil."* rooted in the eternal destiny of death and fear.

Maybe it's time to get personal with God, or rededicate your life. Take a moment and ask Him, in your own words, to deposit His Holy Spirit into your spirit. God made this available through Christ, for those who ask.

Confess your inadequacy to Him, ask forgiveness, and for a cleansing of your heart from negative influence and behaviors. Ask for help to renew your mind with His truths. Approach those you have injured to initiate healing. Forgive those who have injured you.

Moms and dads, maybe it is time to locate your sons

and daughters of any age, and tell them you're sorry and communicate your love to them. It will take time to heal, but take the first step. Ladies and gentlemen, stay chaste in singleness and monogamous in marriage for the benefit of mankind. There are many rewards.

We have our own 9/11 to battle, and the victory is peace, joy, and comfort. These virtues establish unconditional love for our spouses and children, which result in a truly prosperous society. Nonetheless, spiritual terrorism annihilates families, with no "Homeland Security" measures in place. We must pursue the enemy and keep our terror alert in "code red!"

The United States is a country of freedom that almost 300 million people are *blessed* to be a part of. Freedom reigns as brave men and women *unselfishly* serve you and me, in order to provide uninterrupted liberties. Unfortunately, our freedom is not so free, and it is taken for granted by many. There's a price to be paid, and sometimes it comes through bloodshed. *These men and women are our heroes.*

Christ sacrificed Himself, and paid the ultimate price for each one of us, by unselfishly shedding His blood. He didn't do it for Americans alone so they can experience spiritual and emotional freedoms. He died for all colors, races and nations. Americans simply have the privilege to live freely the way God intended for individuals to live, *within His parameters.* If we don't live according to His purpose, the United States will reap havoc as God's patience wears thin.

Our forefathers built America on biblical principles. Today, many people have taken their God-given freedoms in directions never intended, and have put God to the side. It will be an awful day in hell if God decides to throw us to the side because we never knew Him personally.

As we part, may *God Bless America*, you, and your family. Always remember...

*"Another thing you do: You flood the Lord's altar with tears. You weep and wail because he no longer pays attention to your offerings or accepts them with pleasure from your hands. You ask, "Why?" It is because the Lord is acting witness between you and the wife of your youth, because you have broken faith with her, though she is your partner, your wife of your marriage covenant.*

*Has not the Lord made them one? In flesh and in spirit they are his. And why one? Because he was seeking godly offspring. So guard yourself in your spirit, and do not break faith with the wife of your youth.*

*"I hate divorce," says the Lord God of Israel, "and I hate a man's covering himself with violence as well as with his garment," says the Lord Almighty.*

*So guard yourself in your spirit, and do not break faith"* (Malachi 2:13-16).

# TO HIS GLORY PUBLISHING COMPANY, INC.

**463 Dogwood Dr, NW, Lilburn, GA. 30047, U.S.A (770)458-7947**

## Order Form for Bookstores in the USA

Order Date: ...............................................................

Order Placed By: ...............................................................

Address: ...............................................................

By fax: ...............................

By phone: ...............................

City ............................... ST/ZIP ...............................

Phone#: ...............................

Email: ...............................

Purchase Order#: ...............................

Terms: ...............................

Discount ...............................

**Return Policy**: Within 1 Year but not before 90 days

### Title and ISBN#

| Price | Quantity | List Price |
|---|---|---|
|  |  |  |
|  |  |  |
|  |  |  |
|  |  |  |
|  |  |  |
|  |  |  |
|  |  |  |
|  |  |  |
|  |  |  |
|  |  |  |
|  |  |  |
| Shipping Method: |  |  |
| Media |  |  |
| UPS |  |  |
| FedEx |  |  |
| Other (please describe) Total Price: | Total Quantity: |  |

Ship To Address:                    Bill To Address:

TO HIS GLORY PUBLISHING COMPANY, INC. (770) 458-7947 Use Only - Billing Information

# TO HIS GLORY PUBLISHING COMPANY, INC.

463 Dogwood Dr, NW, Lilburn, GA. 30047, U.S.A (770)458-7947

## Order Form for Bookstores in the USA

Order Date:

Order Placed By: _____    By fax: _____

Address: _____    By phone: _____

City _____ ST/ZIP _____    Terms: _____

Phone#: _____

Email: _____    Discount: _____

Purchase Order#: _____

Return Policy: Within 1 Year but not before 90 days

### Title and ISBN#

| Price | Quantity | List Price |
|-------|----------|-----------|
|  |  |  |
|  |  |  |
|  |  |  |
|  |  |  |
|  |  |  |
|  |  |  |
|  |  |  |
|  |  |  |
|  |  |  |
| Shipping Method: |  |  |
| Media |  |  |
| UPS |  |  |
| FedEx |  |  |
| Other (please describe) Total Price: | Total Quantity: |  |

Ship To Address:                    Bill To Address:

TO HIS GLORY PUBLISHING COMPANY, INC. (770) 458-7947 Use Only - Billing Information